DISCOVERIES WITH COACHING

EXECUTIVE AND LIFE COACHING

SNEHASISH DUTTA

First Published in December 2021

ISBN: 978-93-5472-629-3

BLUEROSE PUBLISHERS

www.bluerosepublishers.com

info@bluerosepublishers.com

+91 8882 898 898

Cover Design:

Archita Kumari

Typographic Design:

Ilma Mirza

Distributed by: BlueRose, Amazon, Flipkart

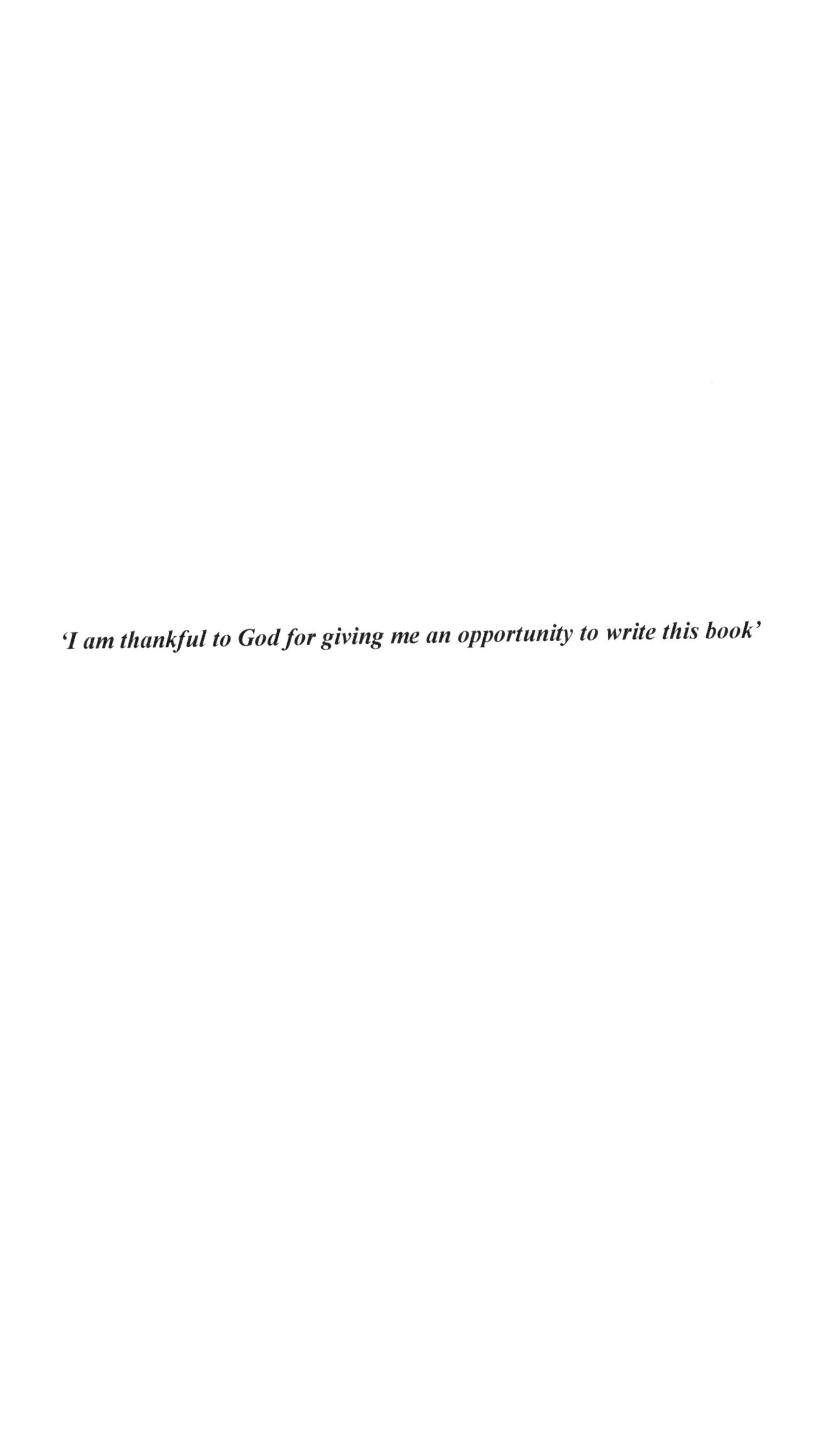

'I am thankful to God for giving me an opportunity to write this book'

DISCOVERIES WITH COACHING

A MUST READ FOR YOUR PERSONAL AND PROFESSIONAL GROWTH

(EXECUTIVE & LIFE COACHING)

FOREWORD BY WORLD NO.1 EXECUTIVE COACH

MR. JOHN MATTONE (STEVE JOBS COACH)

&

COACHING INSIGHTS BY TOP WORLD COACHES

Contents

Introduction

To give back' is not as easy as said. I have been wondering, what could be the best gift to give back to all those who have inspired and taught me and to many, whom I was privileged to inspire, motivate and coach in their life. In all phases of these exchanges, it was not only the perspective for the one who was coached new learning, but also each moment was a new awakening and learning for me as well. What better way it could have been, than to share some thoughts and my discoveries of a new form of guidance called 'COACHING'. In India, many would not be aware of it and would have got exposed to this experiential learning and transformation journey. This book is a small effort meant to give back learnings, which would definitely inspire every individual in their personal and professional growth and journey. Some thoughts, concepts and practice will help everyone in doing things better and faster, which otherwise would have taken longer or lost in the pursuit of dreaming goals only.

Coaching has deep roots in India which I have tried to reflect in the beginning of this book. The more we dig deep into Indian history in ancient texts of the Vedas, the Upanishads, the Bhagwat Geeta, the Ramayana or the Mahabharata, the concepts of coaching and *yog* has high resemblance and inspirations. The modern coaching concepts have quite an inner meaning from the spiritual maturity in the ancient wisdom reflected centuries ago. I am sure it would keep inspiring the world and human beings across the globe with its plethora of knowledge and wisdom for centuries ahead.

Modern coaching and its practice are not limited to few corporates or individuals who are aware and could engage. It's a useful engagement for everyone and rightly recommended for all human being to get exposed to coaching journey at least once in their life.

Yes, coaches are professionals like any other coach in sports, education, health etc. and they are trained, groomed, certified to do their job in the best way to enhance a person's latent potential in a faster and conscious process.

I was exposed to my first coaching about a decade ago and got my first understanding of what formal coaching is all about. Throughout these years, I thank all the coaches who contributed to my understanding, knowledge and specific actions which could assist me do better, aim better and grow better. Coaching started blooming in me and I found it as the next best knowledge I could get after my formal education. Unknowingly, I started coaching others and found that they too are being assisted for their growth. It became a great attraction to me on how can I discover more, what can be the best process for the journey and how it can be of use to me and my family, friends, colleagues, organization and society.

Marshal Goldsmith, John Mattone, Tony Robbins, Sadh guruji , Swamiji's from Ramakrishna Mission , Buddhist Monks started seeding the roots of modern coaching and influenced me in this journey . I got formal training on executive and leadership coaching from John Mattone who was the coach of Steve Jobs, on how to work on both inner and outer core and form a effective process. ICF (International Coaching Federation) various coach programs further enlightened the process with more discoveries and the process continues. ISCP Singapore and ILA Bangalore also became my knowledge partners.

This book would be a compilation of various discoveries and few models which are my own creation like PEIRTR model of coaching conversations, VISIONS coaching process which would definitely give clarity with simplicity of understanding and practice. Various coaching tools gives a self-assessment and discovery. The discoveries start from what and how can coaching fundamentals can help individuals in their personal and professional space. Corporates and Individuals can implement the same at their workplace for enhancing people management skills. Individuals across age groups, be it students, housewives, teachers, coaches and trainers, entrepreneurs, leaders and any professional will surely get few interesting concepts which can help better their productivity and pursuit for goals .

I will be grateful to Mr. John Mattone for the foreword and many thought leaders who have given their insights.

If this book can help even one life for betterment, I would carry the happy feeling of 'giving back'.

Happy reading! Get Coached!

Snehasish Dutta
Coach and Author

About Author

Dr. **Snehasish Dutta** is a Business Leader, Speaker, Executive, Leadership and Life Coach, International Trainer and a research scholar.

He is an ICF (International Coaching Federation) Coach and trained from John Mattone's Academy of Intelligent Leadership. A certified Sales Marketing and Business Professional with doctorate in Business studies, with expertise as Business Coach, DISC – Assessor, NLP for Coaching, Leadership Assessment, Business Effectiveness, Soft-Skills Training etc. He is trained at ISCP-Singapore, Mercuri Goldman, ISB-Society, ASCB, Tata-TMTC, GAAFS- USA, IMC, NLP- European Society, ILA-India. He has coached leaders and individuals across various levels and grooms aspiring coaches. He has represented coaching seminars and is a guest speaker at premier B-Schools.

He has worked across major companies in India last 23 years, namely Tata Motors Ltd, Piaggio Vehicles Ltd, L&T-ECC Ltd, Kirloskar Oil Engines Ltd, BYD.

Winner of several awards including the winner of 2021 MSME best coaching award.

Visit: www.ignitebrainery.com

Acknowledgements

My heartfelt gratitude and sincere acknowledgements for all who have inspired me on the process of writing this book. I would thank the almighty God for building me enough time and patience to complete. I am equally thankful to my wife Dr. Malini Dutta who has seen me coaching and has always asked me to pen down the learnings which can inspire and motivate others. Grateful to her always and to my son Kshitij and daughter Snehalini who kept pushing me to do and also reviewed by progress, all to inspire me.

I am thankful for Tata Group and its several associations of coaching which would have led the early foundations. Thankful to Mr. Marshal Goldsmith whose books have always inspired my leadership thinking. Grateful to Mr. John Mattone who had shared deep insights from Executive and Leadership Coaching, also was kind enough to share his happiness on my writing this book and shared his foreword. Thankful to ISCP Singapore and ILA India.

I am grateful to Ms. Jeanine Bailey-ICF MCC Coach from Australia, Ms. Vijayalakshmi S-ICF MCC Coach from India, Mr. Marco Boschman-ICF MCC Coach from Netherlands, Mr. Kaushik Mohapatra ILA Director from India, Ms. Eva Maria Scheid – Coach and Consultant from Germany for sharing their insights on coaching needs in current times.

I am also grateful to many authors, coaches, ICF, leaders who would have shared their thoughts and processes across various sessions and books.

FOREWORD

COACHING has been always related with excellence in personal and professional growth. Rapidly increasing views of organizations and people, attribute their success, productivity, motivation to coaching experience and look forward further for understanding of their outer and inner core, competencies which can be strengthened, career planning, relationship, finding own purpose, emotional intelligence and many other facets of life. Executive coaching has evolved as a professional process for individual effectiveness for organizational performance while life coaching addresses for personal effectiveness for organizing and excelling (self) across various life challenges and goals.

I met **Snehasish Dutta** in one of our programs, (John Mattone Intelligent Leadership) and found him to be extraordinary on his competencies and knowledge as a coach. I congratulate him for choosing this book **'Discoveries with Coaching'** which I am sure would unravel various dimensions of coaching and how it changes life.

Snehasish has been an avid follower of my books 'Intelligent Leadership', 'Powerful Executive Coaching' and would have reflected on his experience of over 22 years in corporate life to foster new discoveries in coaching excellence. He has a strong belief of inspiring others in his coaching journey and I am sure he would do his best to do it. I understand he has deep insights on how certain discoveries and process, enlighten every individual and gives a high impetus with coaching.

I wish him a great success with his book, would urge readers to read, implement the coaching perspectives in life for their individual success.

John Mattone
World No. 1 Executive Coach
Top 30 Global Gurus of World
(Steve Jobs Executive Coach)
Florida,
USA
August 2021

"Coaching ignites your transformation from a dreamer to a doer"

Coaching Insights by Coaches

Coaching has been at the core of personal and professional growth of an individual. Across countries and professional coaches who have been coaching individuals and would have crossed several hundreds of hours for their growth , I was happy to get feedbacks and some insights from experts and their insights . Let us hear from them .

1.

Jeanine Bailey, ICF - Master Certified Coach (MCC), Australia

Co Director and Co Founder, Empower World (www.empower-world.com)

Certified Coach Supervisor | Coach Mentor

The transformational power of a coach's belief in their client

Professional coaches support clients to uncover their deeper truth and future possibilities going forward. They don't guide or advise their client. Coaches believe their clients know the answers to the questions they ask themselves, which may not be clear to them because of their unconscious ways of thinking, being and doing. The coach supports their client by listening deeply to what they share with them in a psychologically safe place, reflecting back what they notice and hear (spoken and not spoken) and asking thought provoking questions to uncover the client's 'blind spots' in their thinking to create greater conscious awareness and tap into their wisdom and personal truth.

A principle, which underpins the power of coaching, is the belief our clients are naturally creative, resourceful and whole. When coaches adopt this principle, it stops them from rushing in to rescue the client with their own thought of answers. If they do, it limits the client from expanding their thinking and tapping into their inherent wisdom about the way forward with their presenting opportunity or challenge.

This principle may sound may sound good in theory, but a new or even more experienced coach might not practice this principle initially: perhaps guiding and leading their clients according to where their intuition or beliefs think the client should go. And although those ideas might work for the coach, they may not work for the client.

The power of this principle came to reality for me when I was training indigenous women to become professional coaches. A coaching opportunity presented itself when one of the women was incredibly brave and brought in a vulnerable topic. I remember holding the space – allowing silence - after asking an open question after she shared her overwhelming struggle. I didn't come in with another question, or leading questions or words to push down the pain. I trusted this woman, and what she brought into the training for her learning. It felt like everyone was on the edge of their seats as the silence lingered on after asking my question. And all of a sudden, the client's energy and physiology changed into something very powerful. It was like she found her 'mana' (strength and self-worth). She transformed from not knowing the answer for herself to digging deep inside to find an empowering way forward.

When we unpacked the experience, the woman shared it was evolutionary for her. She said, 'It was like we were in our bubble, just the two of us. I could feel the energy from you, Jeanine. I felt you believing in me. And you 'held me' and that allowed me to go into scary places and find my own powerful truth about who I truly am.'

Based on this experience, I too felt transformed as a coach. I know now, if I hold the space for my clients and see them as naturally creative, resourceful and whole, my client will find the answer within.

If we see our client as broken or need mending, that energy is potentially being transferred to your client. So, it's about being mindful about how we show up, the principles we adhere to and who we are being as a coach to support our client to identify and create powerful changes. So, if you are a new - or a more experienced coach, let go of wanting anything for your client and trust they'll find their own way. A client may not come up with their answer straight away. It might take an hour or a day or a few weeks or months' time. If you champion them and acknowledge they are incredibly capable and creative - that they will find their way when they're ready - you are supporting your client to recognise they are naturally creative, resourceful and whole.

2.

Vijayalakshmi S, ICF MCC and EMCC – India

Master Coach & Mentor (ICF & EMCC) Coaching Evangelist President – ICF Chennai Charter Chapter Founding Volunteer Leader – CoachesForYou

Navigating life in our present times – with some help! The last 18 months since the advent of the Covid-19 pandemic, has brought to the fore the reality of a general state of confusion, inertia and loneliness. No one seems to have the answers to many seemingly basic questions, and many of our old ways of working & being had to undergo overnight changes. These times have been undoubtedly been hard times of resilience & personal growth for humanity, sparing none. However, it has also provided us an opportunity to take a hard look at the lives we are leading and about what choices we need to make, going forward.

These are times when we could all do with a bit of help! While this help is available in many forms, from people in our lives and in the form of friends, family and colleagues, it is also available professionally. It's the time for helping professions such as Coaching to show up, to support people to navigate through confusing and challenging times.

Coaching, simply put is a partnership that allows one to realize their personal & professional goals, explore and maximize one's full potential. And there could be no better time than now for coaches to partner with clients to help them navigate cross-roads of their life. Be it in the areas of health & wellness, conflicts, career, relationships or life in general, coaching can help! The pandemic has provided an opportunity for us to consider "resetting" our lives, and coaching is a powerful way to facilitate such resets, simply because the client finds their own answers to existential questions through a process of deep reflection, enquiry and dialogue, in a safe setting.

As a professional practicing Coach, the last 1.5 years has provided me an opportunity to support & serve people from different walks of life, ages, cultures & geographies, both commercially and probono. It has left me feeling fortunate about the real difference my contribution is making in small ways to heal the world that seems hurt. I would like to leave you with a message - If you are navigating a challenging phase that seems over-whelming or simply wish to work on a different direction in your life, you don't have to go it alone – give Professional Coaching a try!

3.

Marco Buschman, ICF - Master Certified Coach (MCC), CTPC , CPCC , Netherlands

Managing Partner COURIUS and author of 'The Connection Quotient'

In one of the coaching courses I conduct, I invite participants to ask each other the question: What is your biggest dream? This always produces some special moments. First there's the sense of confusion as the participants think, what is my biggest dream? Do I actually have one? But gradually, as more people have asked them the question, and everyone has heard other people's answers, you can feel the positive energy and mutual inspiration that is being created.

The participants make contact or re-connect with what is important to them. And they immediately make contact with others at a deeper level. Almost everyone is grateful they did the exercise and acknowledge that the question should be asked more often. And yet, when I ask them how often they ask a colleague or a friend this question, the answer is typically: "Well, never, actually." Why is it that we hardly ever put this question to ourselves and others? Probably because we are so caught up in the process of delivery. We act as Human Doings, being tasks and results oriented and adding value to the process and our customers. Keep doing that I would say. And, next to being a Human Doing, also be a Human Being. Life's not only about being successful, it's also about feeling fulfilled. It's not only about chasing ambitions, it's also about living your dreams. It's not only about earning money, it's also about experiencing happiness. Etcetera.

This is where coaching fits in. The process of coaching helps (or challenges) you to look inwards. Not only to reflect on your actions, but also to introspect on your behaviour. What defines who you are and drives your actions? Amongst others your thoughts, your emotions, your personal values, your (limiting) beliefs, your fears, your desires, etc. It takes courage to explore this inner world.

Are you ready to look inwards and to open up? To live your bigger game? To have courageous conversations and to act on the insights? If the answer to these questions is yes, then reach out to a coach and be ready to being a powerful Human Doing AND Human Being. **Enjoy your journey!**

4.

Kaushik Mohapatra, Founder & Director , Indian Leadership Academy , India

International Leadership Trainer, Speaker, Master Coach , Author

Lead Like a Coach

Did you know that Coaching is the most powerful tool for self-development in today's world?

Did you know that Coaching is the least used Leadership skill?

Did you know we can Model someone's Behaviour and accelerate our growth exponentially?

Welcome to the world of Coaching.

My name is Kaushik Mahapatra, a Master Coach, Leadership Thinker, Top Selling Author and the Founder of Indian Leadership Academy. In my 25 Years of work experience, i have been exposed to coaching for last 12 years both for my self-development and my team's growth and it has been an absolute game changer for me.

In the last decade, Coaching has evolved and has yielded better results than training and mentoring. However, Lot of people still can't differentiate between coaching and mentoring and are not able to reap the benefits of coaching.

For every leader or manager or someone who manages a team, coaching can certainly give you a new dimension and a new way of living both personally and professionally. Both Professional Coaching and Life coaching are getting extremely popular throughout the world and everyone is looking up to a coach in their life for getting clarity, continuous growth, Success, prosperity and ultimately find out why we do what we do.

Core coaching skills like empathy, curiosity and listening has become the most sought-after attributes for a Great leader and has helped good leaders transition from Good to Great.

In the next decade, I foresee that Education industry is going to be completely reformed through usage of coaching. Teachers, Professors and Educators would be exposed to coaching and it would bring a new dimension to students' growth, empowerment and success. Coaching would be a great tool for teachers to improve their ability to reflect it would assist them to understand why some students don't apply what they learn. Moreover, Teaching would be much more rewarding due to coaching as it is much more personalized for students. So we should not be surprised if coaching is added to the curriculum in schools and universities and students are getting exposed to coaching at a very young age.

Keep exploring the world of coaching !

5.

Eva Maria Scheid. **Consulting, Coaching & Training, Germany**

evamariascheid.de | https://linkedin.com/in/evamariascheid

How working with the Inner Family Systems (IFS) coaching approach can help reaching your personal and career goals.

Imagine this exemplary situation:

A part of you is longing for that dream job. And your credentials are really great so that your name regularly gets listed on the short list of hiring companies. However, another part of you seems to torpedo your plan from a hidden place. So far, none of the job interviews has led to the desired success: your dream job repeatedly goes to someone else.

Let’s look at a second example:

Your co-worker and you are getting along well and you are very productive as a team. However, there is this one thing your co-worker does regularly which seems to drive you crazy: She arranges a specific date and time for a client meeting for both of you without checking with you. And while your diary is free and the date and time are generally speaking ok, it still triggers a certain unhelpful reaction of yours. While you know that the reaction is unhelpful, you are not able to change your behavior.

What power is at work in these situations?

Let’s assume the parts with the unhelpful reactions in the above examples are stuck in the past and thus act from that perspective. They had good reasons for developing their views and beliefs back then. Their reactions were most likely needed to overcome certain difficult situations. But it seems those very same views and beliefs are now dysfunctional.

So how can you change the outcome?

When you embark on a transformative and enriching journey with the Inner Family Systems approach, you will get to know your parts (the members of your inner family). As you start to understand the individual story of each part and its positive intention, transformative and game changing outcomes are possible. Parts will most likely change over time and redefine their role.

Let’s revisit the examples.

In the first example, the torpedoing part could evolve into a part that helps the Self via ensuring the new job is really a good fit. Maybe it performs a thorough due diligence and helps finding the best option. It could also be that the torpedoing part wants to protect you from shame and thus doesn’t want you to act out. Understanding those old feelings and leaving the shame behind could enable a strong self-expression. You never know up front. It is really an individual transformation.

In the second example, the part demonstrating the unhelpful behavior might be in strong need for autonomy. The transformed part might be able to ensure an adequate level of autonomy in a calm and relaxed manner.

We are talking about a discovery journey with amazing and often unexpected insights.

A single session can already make an initial difference for a certain situation. A handful of sessions makes it more sustainable. Giving your core Self more air-time and working with all the members of your inner family (maybe 12-15) will take some time.

Chapter - 1

Introduction to the world of Coaching :

Came across the word **"Coaching"** quite early in life with early childhood when parents use to coach and guide like a very typical Indian orthodox family who would like to impart the best of academic and spiritual knowledge early in their children. Years passed and happen to hear these often in school, college, coaching classes and then the MBA days, corporate life, PhD sessions, maturing in my training sessions and so on.

It was early 2000 and happen to go through unending sessions of corporate grooming and knowledge upliftment and 'coaching' became quite synchronous with appraisals and HR domain specific. My affinity towards this word became subconsciously within me. I started being closely following subjects, words, people and their practices and observed **"what's coaching"** and what's need and implications.

With years post that and the utility attached with changes in people behavior, their habits, their responses to situation and evolving to their best, slowly made me fall in awe of this word and made me practice this across my clients with a definitive success and positive change.

My purpose here is to look back at Coaching, which is such a beautiful and strong tool, having capacity to change and transform lives and contribute towards Igniting your own core and imparting the same to others. I have tried to decipher the knowledge and would like to add principles and process for effective application of coaching which transforms and ignites a **'new you'** and share the discoveries.

Coaching emerges from its historical roots. Parents, teachers, society playing an important role in the early stages of coaching in anyone's life.

Origins of Coaching: While professional coaching has a known history of origination around 1980's with Thomas Leonard – an American financial planner. Leonard observed that his clients, though emotionally stable and hardly needing therapy, wanted more from him than just the usual tips on how to invest and safeguard their incomes. His observation skills of human behaviour to different stimuli yet he didn't want to be overlapped with therapists, mentors, psychologist or consultants.

Coaching in early Indian scriptures and religious books:

Coaching is not new in India and strangely has been with Indian history last so many centuries. From the Vedas, the Upanishads, the Ramayana, the Mahabharata we have read of the 'Guru-Shishya Parampara' which has been one of the oldest coaching approaches by human civilisation. In today's world too, we have world's best coaches with best 'Gurus'. The Kings would practice sending their children to 'Gurus' in ashramas, which were schools of wisdom. Kings also had the *raj gurus* which means royal teachers who would coach kings for any situation. Speaking with reference to ancient yogic teachings in India, human being has inner mind is referred as 'Antahkarna- Inner Being'. We need to understand the beautiful manifestation of the mind which is defined having 4 quadrants.

- *Ahankara* – it focusses on the self-ego. Ego which becomes ever focussed on 'me' and 'I' becomes quite detrimental for coaching process growth.
- *Chitta* – Mind thinking about memories of past or future and visualizing
- *Manas* – Refers to mind and this is related to how mind manifests the memory and recognises with sensory organs.

- *Budhi* – Intellect, this records all the memories, process the same and let the intellect decide on what's right or wrong.

This also reflects in ancient Buddhism which depicts the school of thought of reading mind and its functions which later becomes the core of coaching.

Lord Krishna as Coach : I wondered the early civilisation would have any such hints in India, like the ancient origination of Vedas or Yoga or Meditation in Indian mythology beyond 5000 BC. One of the inspiring acknowledgements of Coaching which always charges me was the reference to Indian holy scripture of 'Bhagavad Gita', a 700-verse epic during Mahabharata dated around the same time frame. The Gita is set in a narrative framework of dialogue between Pandava prince Arjuna and his guide and charioteer Lord Krishna, an avatar of Lord Vishnu. Arjuna is filled with moral dilemma and despair about the violence and death the war will cause in the battle against his own kin. He wonders if he should renounce and seeks Krishna's counsel, whose answers and discourse constitute the Bhagavad Gita. While my discourse hovers around, Lord Krishna who actually incarnates as 'Coach Krishna' and leads Arjuna to understand and unravel his ethical, philosophical and spiritual dilemmas right in the battle field when Arjuna almost decides to give up on the first day and later wins the battle fighting good over evil against his own kin. Lord Krishna artistically coaches Arjuna of all his queries and takes him to uncover his decisions in his own consciousness. Here's are few take away which were in Sanskrit which has been guiding humanity for ages and I am sure would continue for ages, also it makes so much sensible considering the modern coaching practices.

"Karmanye vadhikaraste ma phalesu kadachana

Ma Karmaphalehturbhurma te sangostvakarmani"

You have the right to perform your duties , but you are not entitled to the fruits of your actions . Never consider to the cause of results of your activities, nor be attached to the inaction.

The whole teaching behind has been to enforce right and correct actions which focuses on actions (high surety) for results (unsure) and not the vice-versa.

"Matrasparsastu Kaunteya itosnasukhdukhkahdaha

Agamapayino nityas-tans-titishasva bharata"

O Kaunteya (son of Kunti, referring Arjuna) contact with the sense objects creates hot and cold, pleasure and pain, they are transient, they come and go. Bear with them, O Bharata.

Tough times come and go, learn to tolerate and prepare for the next, don't get easily affected by it. Nothing is permanent in this world. You are the master of your own response, situation isn't in your control, what you can control and change is your response to the situation, your own stimuli management.

There are many such versions and lessons out of these scriptures which are now being understood with modern co-relation and has been a part of top B Schools and management sessions. The entire communication of Lord Krishna with Arjuna was nothing but a huge coaching book and each *sloka* reflects modern coaching.

Coaching synonymous with sports : Coaching has been quite synonymous to sports. Coach and sports go very familiar to most people. Origins date back to 1860's in England when the athletes were trained by external help. Slowly people who had experience, knowledge of that particular sport started grooming sports men and women across all sports and it gained the popularity of the deliverable of the coach and the impact it created on the performance of the player or the team.

So what's new in this book –

Humans across globe have one common characteristic. Dreams and Challenges. We are blessed with brains to speak and use reasoning. We have emotions and we are reactive to various stimuli. We interact and communicate, we are rational, we display conscience, we exhibit our feelings, we think, we decide between good and bad, we are driven by our conscience, we face hardships, we strive to find ways and means survive, we win and we lose, we plan, we commit mistakes, we are social and learn from each other, we cry and we laugh.

In modern times, everyone would be driven by various dreams and goals, face challenges and obstacles, would seek how better and quicker a path can be drawn for winning over the hurdles and continuously evolve for their growth. **Coaching** has been one of finest discoveries and people management skill for addressing these subjects, work towards a better life and grow individually.

I have tried to make Coaching simpler on how everyone can be coached and each one can coach. While we aren't new to coaching, often we may mix other concepts of mentoring, consulting and not lead to real coaching dialogues. As per latest publication of ICF, Coaching effectiveness has been as high as 70%-90%. That simply means if the discussion is provoked with positive and constructive thoughts which have a futuristic outlook, gives much better '***change***' than just telling or saying.

Getting committed to the personal development, development of your peer, organisation, family, friends and contacts with focus internally for your own growth. I have tried to incorporate emotional intelligence (EQ) and your Spiritual Intelligence (SQ) and how they overall contribute to the behavioural changes. Performance in corporate professionals, just cannot be driven by pure appraisals, KPI or KRAs. Coaching integrates uncovering true values, producing high levels of self-discovery and aligning towards the goal which merges somewhere between the personal and professional achievements without which, it cannot be optimised.

Coaching I call as Inner Engineering and Igniting your own potentials which may have got subdued over a period of time owing to various circumstances. It reflects on the intra transpersonal psychology, which creates much better will, determination and preparedness for the responsibility.

There is no right or wrong process of coaching. Each personality shows and unravels plethora of human behavioural panorama and needs individual management. Unravelling of true potential beautifully merges between the 'self 'and 'them/they/external'. The need for evolution in each individual overall contributes to the growth of overall perspective, organisation's larger vision and develops the collective strength. Coaching brings on board the spirit of own performance with lot clarity about own goals, testing its hypothesis, planning a sure tested road map with checks at intermittent gaps and leading to definitive success formula with a clear timeline in mind.

I am sure, this book would be igniting a framework of self-engineering and address students, individuals, corporate professionals and leaders, housewives looking to restart with some goals, new and experienced coaches, mentors, HR leaders, etc.

A quick example: - A leader whom I was coaching was looked at strategic senior roles by his organisation. He was dominant and would rumble on people management although he would be focussed towards goals. While his manager and organisational pressure was towards the internal achievements, coaching came in handy to make him aware of what's missing for a larger role, what's need to be plugged to ensure better team management and emerge as a leader who is a role model. Continuous sessions over months helped him to realise and change his behaviour and project himself differently. A deep core understanding and planning with a definitive road map shaped him. Had it not for the coaching assignment, he would have never unlearned and replaced with what's more effective and needed for senior management roles.

What is Coaching?

Focus on Future Constructive Development, It's a GPS navigation of Self from Now to Then.

The Oxford Dictionary meaning 'the process of training somebody, to play a sport, to do a job better or to improve a skill'

And a Coach is 'a person who trains a person or team in sport'

While the historical origination is quite synonymous with sports, the literal meaning has been redefined with the changing dynamics in people management across fields, domains, industry, society.

Coaching – it's a high impact interactive dialogue, where coach triggers the beliefs, attitudes, habits and his response to various situations and provokes him/her on a constructive, thoughtful journey which has a definitive road map for growth. Its inspiring, future paced, and digs down to unravel your best potential talents and shape them towards a goal for success. The relationship is built on trust, confidentiality and support. The coachee does require to find his/her best answers to his current and future challenges, which is stimulated or provoked by the coach. The process is always paced over a period of time as it needs to sink in with the behavioural changes in emotional, physiological responses and needs to have a 'habit mutation'.

Timothy Gallwey, a Harvard scholar and tennis player and expert, coined it simple: 'The Inner Game of Tennis' harping on the essence of coaching. Coaching is unlocking people's potential to maximise their own performance. It's so simple to understand, imagine a parent showing his/her child how to walk , takes few steps with him and then leaves the hand to ensure the child balances enough to take the first few steps of his/her life . Referring to The Bhagwad Gita again, Lord Krishna was all powerful and all the mighty to fight the Kauravas in the battlefield of Mahabharata, he was alone the supreme almighty to defeat all, yet he didn't take up weapons , he kept on coaching Arjuna , led his chariot , coached him on evil and virtuous and led him to the victory of war , victory of right , victory of mankind . Coaching was passed on for generations and would constantly be needed in everyone's life to constantly lead the situation . Its quite nice to also understand that the best of coaches in the world, also has a coach , sometimes he is his own coach .

Who is a Coach? – A person is trusted, trained and competent person who works with the human potential, his/her psychology and captures the purpose and need of the coachee. Set the right perspective to derive the best in potential for professional and personal growth, ignites awareness, associates with coachee to find his/her solutions with increased confidence and commitment.

Understanding Coaching better :

Ask Questions and Co-Create based on Client's Knowledge and Experience

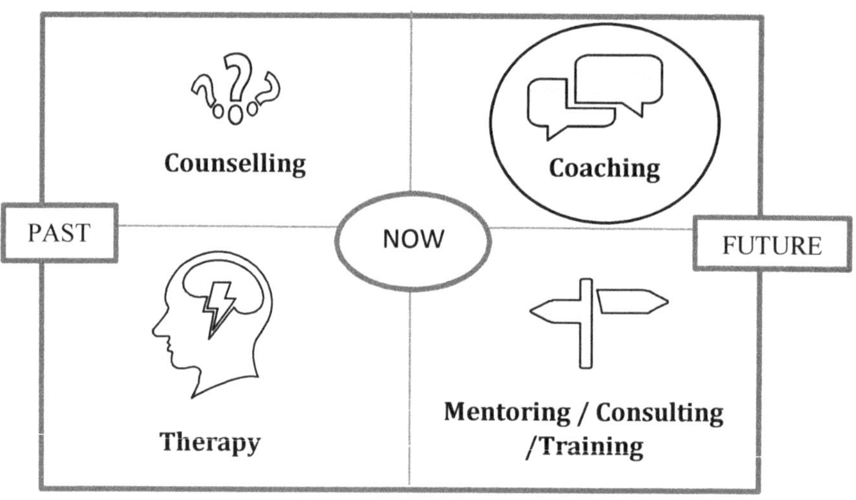

Tell Client and Co-Create based on Provider's Knowledge and Experience

The Coaching quadrant above is a simple illustration of the entire subject. The process is simplified to **'ask questions and co-create based on client's knowledge and experience'** and is **'future focused'**.

While counselling dwells on past which asks relevant questions and brings the coachee to the current zone of present, where he/she would be out from a trauma/bitter past and would be better now.

Mentoring, consulting and training are **'tell'** operations which are downloaded from experts, consultants and expected to copy / put ahead a replica of the actual experience, session, methods etc .

As a coach, I value the top quadrant of coaching as a growth zone in individual, where he/she is self-driven with a navigation guide. He/She has own control and propels towards the outcome using its best resources. A sustained growth and development is achieved which stays forever in the individual as it shapes its habit , defines his/her responses for future similar situations .

SUPERVISION, MENTORING AND COACHING:

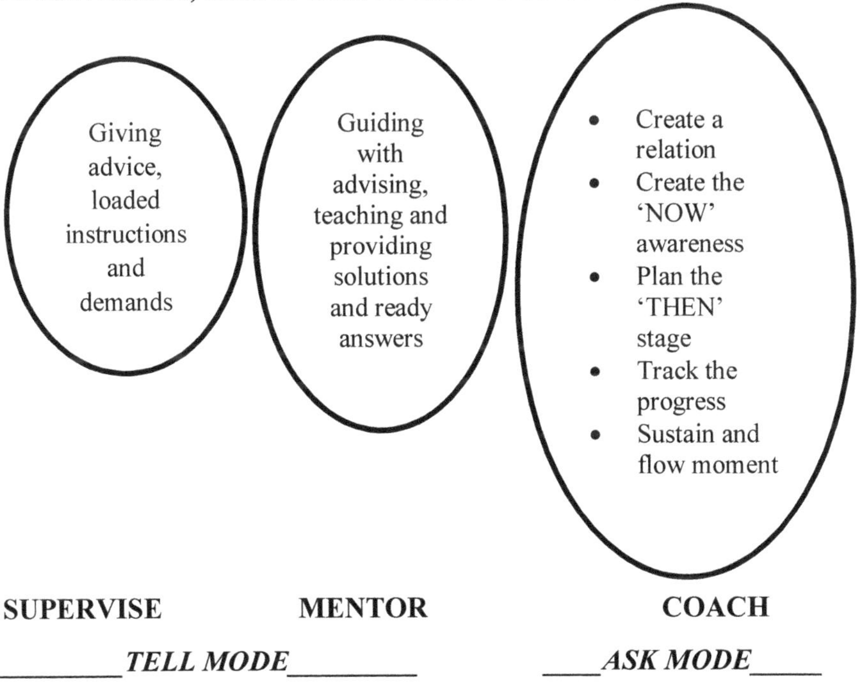

Giving advice, loaded instructions and demands

Guiding with advising, teaching and providing solutions and ready answers

- Create a relation
- Create the 'NOW' awareness
- Plan the 'THEN' stage
- Track the progress
- Sustain and flow moment

SUPERVISE **MENTOR** **COACH**

_________TELL MODE________ ***____ASK MODE_____***

"Discovering SELF, is the biggest learning before you coach others"

Discoveries with Coaching :

Chapter - 2

How do we discover ourselves?

In my early stages of coaching understanding, I asked my coach as to what's coaching and how do we discover various traits, behavior of people and lead them on the coaching journey.

Interestingly, I was told, that , we will step over and learn how to discover others gradually but first the effort has to be deep with yourself on discovering yourself in every possible way .

Discovering yourself 100% opens your knowledge and understanding of discovering others.

How do you discover yourself then?

My coach had a simple answer.

Write a paragraph about yourself

I wondered as to how this will help me discover, I can always write 200-300 words on this. That was where he said as ***write it daily and every time you write it has to be different***. This exercise went on few days and then he asked me to reflect on what I wrote the first time to what I could pen down the last time.

This itself was a discovery. The words, sentences and the essence was going deeper and deeper and I was trying to dig into my habits , my behavior , my likes & dislikes , my reactive and proactive understanding , my perception of people and their behavior etc . The more I start writing as a habit everyday about myself , I realized, subconsciously I have started knowing others better and clearer . This is the discovery phase which opens your coaching start .

"Unless you know yourself well, you may not know others well"

Coaching is a discovery process, each meeting with others, not only opens doors of new vistas but also reflects on various ways on our own understanding and mastering it. The questions, responses and answers to various questions is deep within us as an answer, this process slowly opens it for your understanding.

Coaching Tool – 1 Let us discover- Self Discovery

Please write a paragraph about yourself

____

____

____

____

____

____

____

____

____

____

____

____

____

____

Harnessing Potential: Any coaching discussion or assignment has to be have a complete clarity on the coachee's potentials and the need for what they have to express it. Coachee has to be coached on his potential strengths, his core competencies and not on his performance or current status. This is a classic flaw in the appraisal cycles where performance wise boxes are mapped rather than potential wise. In classic corporate culture people who tend to be low on performance are mapped with coaches which makes coachee first being jittery as why he/she has been assigned a coach. In contrast, organization across their structure irrespective of performance needs coaching for growth. Similarly, any individual needs to be coached on his latent potential.

For example, I coached a mid-level manager when he was in dilemma of his role change within the organization. During coaching, he started exhibited strengths which he may have overlooked or underestimated, soon he exhibited his own career road map which not only looked at shorter time lines but on larger time lines of career. Finally, he could open up and get going fast on his career ladder initially within organization, later outside it.

The catalyst of anxiety and psychological unrest, owing to certain triggers can surely take a coachee if not a super natural development graph, but surely better than had he/she not undergone the coaching sessions

When do you use coaching?

Frankly anybody and everybody needs coaching at some point of time and I strongly recommend 1-2 session for all human beings irrespective of nations, work, age or positions. However, we will list a few:

- Appraisals
- Cascading of organization's mission and vision or common tasks
- Relationships, Team camaraderie
- Solving any problem, personal or professional
- Delegation
- Role enhancement
- Mergers and acquisitions
- Cultural grooming during change of country/religion or immigration

- Crisis management
- And many more ....

Who needs Coaching – Only a simple answer-"EVERYONE"

Consider the following situations:

- My work life and family life are messing up.
- I have a great team, but all are not focused
- My relationship with my senior is not great
- I am yet to start the job of my dreams
- I feel I am not doing what I wanted to always do
- My children seem to be not much respectful
- What do I do when I start living alone?
- My job has got affected in pandemic, what should I now plan
- We have an idea, no one is ready to invest
- My manager does not appreciate my work
- Some other companies are catching up to our USPs, are we left behind?
- Organization needs a drive, I am seeing a gap
- I am worried about my health
- I know my goal

Many of the above questions are quite common and may be asked by all of us and then we start our own pursuit for finding an answer. We would be fortunate to find the answer but may not be sure about it . Sometimes, we may feel lonely with our decision and drive alone assuming success. Such situations and many such is the birth of rightful conversation with a coach.

Often, I had come across as to clients saying that I don't know 'what's troubling me, but surely its troubling me". Frankly, any human being would be having multiple facades of his/her life across his/her personal or professional front. Often its ignored as it might sound 'not right to discuss' or 'it's too silly or confidential' or 'if I am not able to solve, how can Coach help me?' .... such right questions and queries are cleared in several interactions and that's where it says that a proper conversation always results at high efficacy for change, sometimes 80-90%

Why does Coaching works most of the time – TAGE

1. **T** – its starts with the **Trust** which is to be developed between the coach and coachee . Many times, the whole coaching process fails in absence of it. With trust building, the two individuals become a **Team** and work jointly
2. **A – Accountability** exhibited by the coachee with coach provoking, challenging and giving the coachee a larger perspective of actions.
3. **G – Goals** – The entire effort gone in the continuous arriving at the right goal, becomes an ownership of coachee. Coach helps to continuously dwell on intermittent smaller goals for the achievement of the larger goals.
4. **E – Experience –** Coach is able to understand, gauge and assist the coachee drive with his/her expertise towards faster arrival towards the goal. Coach satisfaction is only when coachee is able to arrive at the success door.

What do you achieve with Coaching: There are numerous subjects which the coach and coachee work and these are the common assignments which are undertaken?

- Areas of Improvement – a typical appraisal
- Business target planning, goal planning
- Converting a weakness to strength
- Prioritization at work or life
- Planning better work – life balance
- Career planning
- Achievement planning – it can be sales, turnover , global footprint etc.
- 360* turnaround strategy
- Delegation of organization's larger vision across all departments

- How to manage diversified workforce – in case of mergers, role elevation
- Personal growth and development plan
- Evolving with crisis – like Covid Management at Work
- Individual contribution enhancement

Many more ….

So how does a Coach – Coaches: -

Coaching is not done abruptly and suddenly. At least few pre-coaching sessions (normally called the chemistry sessions) are planned in advance. On a business or executive coaching session contracted by a organization, there should be Business – HR – Coachee pre meetings done, together and individually. A coach understanding of the complete perspective is mandatory for any coaching conversation. Often coachee's perspective differs from organization's perspective and vice-versa. A clear addressable coaching objective is set and mutually planned in advance. A coaching agreement to follow. In case of Individual assignment, often one to one pre meeting with addressable subjects discussed and agreed upon. An effective coaching session spreads over few sessions over weekly, monthly schedule and planned jointly. Coach plans the session with a clear session goals or outcomes and takes the conversation on a constructive, thought-provoking journey. The effort is that when coachee plans a larger goal, coach plans and designs support with what can be smaller and tiny achievements which at every step can be seen as a milestone of success. The coach brings out the hidden potential and uncovers strategy and leads to a path which may be challenging but is inspired at all steps with depth of discussion, test of failures, realization of the goals and celebrating each win in the course. Coach is trained, expert in his management of the immediate perspective of the coachee and exactly asks the 'relevant questions' to see 'great answers' coming by. (We will dwell upon in details on relevant questions and answers)

What's the role of Coachee: - Most Importantly a coachee has to bring in?

"A mindset which is present with a commitment to think, discover and grow"

As a professional coach, I found a major difference is purely a mindset which needs to focus. Most of clients with a clear focus of thinking, discovering, planning, committing and taking action has greater success rates and faster. While many coaching sessions, coachee slowly falls in the same process even if initial sessions may be not in the same pace. ***Always remember any coaching session is in service of the coachee and not the coach***. It's the success of coachee which counts, coach would primarily be contracted and would be paid before.

Coach – Coachee relationship:

Coaching relationship between the coach the coachee is very profound. It's a relationship where both exhibit high levels of confidentiality, collaboration, mutual trust and respect, have a camaraderie like partners and both share a common vision of growth in the coachee's status. Often referred as a great bonding, beautiful chemistry, building the environment of coachee's development in the entire process. Compatibility of the coach and coachee is an important criterion of the coach selection process and goes well with a pre-understanding of each other. Coachee would like to give his/her view point, areas of concerns and what is that he/she is looking ahead for their growth. While coach would be seeing the matching intent, coachability factors, backgrounds and the time period expected. In case the coaching assignment is sourced by organization, then how effective is the desired output, measured with respect to coachee's view point and desired growth from organization's perspective becomes the essential key.

Goal of any Coaching conversation: -

Our most familiar understanding that of Indian Cricket, where the coach helps a person to improve his cricket or his strokes by observing, diagnosing, providing feedback, demonstrating, and setting a new style, technique best fitting him and outlines the step-by-step routines and targets. The goal is chosen by the client, but the coach functions as an expert and trainer, often being quite coercive in that process. Such coaching can also involve broader goals, more holistic approach. Often coachee discovers new dimensions, styles and better adaptions to the similar bowling.

I refer to one video being streamed in a session, where a mother is grooming his blind child to handle the situations of life independently. Mother sees the child at many a times with near risk situation, yet she does not let the child feel she is around. Sounds, words, smell, touch and hands become the eyes and the ears of making the sound respond these stimuli, coaches the child behave and grow more independently than otherwise. Here, mother acts a coach who is just focussed to ensure the child grows up independently and slowly introduces various techniques and process to make the child learn and master. Here the child who is a coachee would see the initial periods as very challenging and difficult to may be give it up, but once the smaller achievements done , celebration and success repeats . The goal of being independent is achieved.

The Goal of any coaching session is therefore clear, making the coachee reach the success and thereafter he/she independently treads on the path for repeat success. Knowing 'NOW .... TO THERE'

Critical to know with the coachee is the basic discovery process to know the "NOW" situation and "HERE" and to tread the path "TO THERE". Many assumptions, over or under judgements prevail to figure the real situation. What may be an assumption may be incorrect, or underplayed? A clear clarity of these defines the entire journey of coaching. Many coaching assignments may be not going ahead till 'to there' status as it's the unclear understanding of 'now' and the required inertia which pushes to the destination for success. The whole effort narrows to finding the 'now' and reality and the 'to there' as the goal. The process in between is the coaching drive. Once the start and end is known, then the momentum is so strong that the coachee independently moves on. Coach success is to ensure the momentum is enough so that coachee drives it with coach or without the coach. Finding current reality and status is often the biggest discovery and shaping the goal of the destination is the biggest conclusion which automatically drives internal commitment.

How Coaching is effective vs. conventional mechanisms:

Coaching effectiveness				
	Only Telling and Directing	**Telling with Demonstrating on how to be done**	**Telling, Demonstrating and experiencing the process**	**Evoking awareness and facilitating process with direction set by doer**
Action within 21 days	30-50%	50-60%	60-80%	100%
Action 90-120 days	>10%	>30%	>60%	>95%

To elaborate, the practices for Life or Executive coaching is no more on the 'tell mode'. More and more it is being looked at empowering the DOER the results have been long lasting. To summarize the above:

- Only Telling and Directing – DOES NOT WORK – AVOID
- Telling with Demonstrating on how to be done – LOW RESULTS

- Telling, Demonstrating and experiencing the process – SOME VISIBLE RESULTS – YET NOT SUSTAINABLE, SHORT - TERM PLAN
- Evoking awareness and facilitating process with direction set by doer- MOST EFFECTIVE AND SHOULD BE PRACTICED

Let's see it from a simple example – Parents would like to see their children successful in their careers and life , from childhood, children are subjected to tell mode and may not see all advices , direction worth doing and may not be doing in practice . It's not about the direction, it's the way it's being guided. Let's see a conversation:

- "Do this, this is good, I know it"
- "This looks good, let's try and do it together"
- "This looked good, we enjoyed doing together, try again"
- "It looks good, what can we do together to make it happen"

The entire conversation shapes differently in the conversation from 1st sentence to last. In practice, ALL conversations can be shaped and modified with correct way of asking and not telling, commanding or just directing. The overall impacts changes dramatically and is sustained.

Inner core of coaching :

The observation can help discover the inner core .

'Why aren't you performing at your work?'

The question would have various answers . The moment it is asked , coachee would be defensive and not be coming forthright . It can push him/her back , feel nervous and anxious , coachee would be talking less , sometimes even look downwards and do not have an eye contact . Answers may be 'yes I am doing good' or 'oh..i will do better' or 'yes' or 'no' or 'give me one more chance'.

Now the question is reframed as :

'What is stopping you to do better in work?'

'What challenges are you facing now?'

'Can you tell me more on where you could not perform?'

'Is there any support which can assist you to better perform?'

'How can you plan better to perform at work?'

'What are your plans now to be a better performer?'

All the above questions are insightful. It does not make the coachee nervous but allows him/her to think for a moment, grasp what is not working correct, focus on exact things what is going wrong and needs correction. This also brings in the accountability and responsibility to handle better the situation henceforth.

The questions arouse awareness , thoughts and provokes creative outcome. It also compels the coachee to exhibit better plans and actions which can bring a change .

Hence the inner core of coaching is to focus on creating awareness and bring responsivity and responsibility

Somebody asked a question, does coaching always work? What happens if sometime the result isn't achieved?

Coaching is a JOURNEY; the process and journey is important. After having clarity on the coaching process, the deliberation is all about how do you find the new current reality and set a goal plan. Knowing the goal, knowing the action plan and focussing on these actions is sure to lead to success. It's not about the goal anymore once visualised, it's the effort thereafter on the journey and the smaller milestones achievement. Hence, the achievement here would be better or more than what a coachee would otherwise not plan or do in the similar focussed plans or actions.

Corporates are growing and changing for good of the organisation and the employee management process.

What would be an ideal management system look like?

IDEAL MANAGEMENT SHIFT	
Normal Traditional Management	**Coaching Management**
Manage only results	Create long term sustainable results
Control Employee actions	Empowering Employee
Focus on weakness / Pin at Areas of Improvement	Focus on strengths, Majority focus on making strengths stronger
Fear and consequences	Risk appetite with stronger participation
Authoritative	Delegation and bonding
Solve issues short term	Prevent issues with long term
Listen to employee	Listen, understand and actively engage
Assignment to employee given randomly	Proactively engage to fit to employee strength and redefine assignment
Source of approval	Collaboration and resource maximisation nodal unit.
More time to work only	Manage actively work-life-fun and creativity

Coaching thoughts come from:

- Parents and parenting
- Sports
- Phycology
- Nature
- Science
- Philosophy
- Mythology and ancient scriptures
- Modern teaching
- Communication
- Great leaders and their principles
- Wisdom

The above sources clearly show the origin of the various thoughts and birth of the modern coaching methods.

Broad understanding of the types of Coaching:

1. **Executive Coaching** – Leadership planning, goal setting, delegation, personal management with appraisals, productivity, etc
2. **Personal Coaching** – it can be across topics of relationships, personal goals, stress and work-life management, priorities, spirituality, emerging from crisis etc
3. **Career Coaching** – It focusses on individual plans for career development, management, skills and methods, long term planning etc
4. **Business Coaching** – Targets and business turnover, vision and mission planning, diversifications, branding etc.
5. **Health, Spiritual Coaching** – focus of physical well-being , better life skills, meaning and purpose etc.

Some associates, corporates asked on whether we should have internal coaches from organization or should hire external coaches. Here is a quick summary of the possible advantages, disadvantages.

INTERNAL COACHES	EXTERNAL COACHES
• More aware of the domain knowledge but may not be aware of the coaching process • Greater knowledge of company culture , vision • May not have exposure • Internal Org. focused • Coaching skills , tools , assessments may be missing on the knowledge • Would be constrained on time • May be biased or judgmental and may tend towards mentoring • Confidentiality can be a challenge • Detailed follow up or progression with the coachee may be missing • Coachee do not open up 100% • Practically no cost	• Certified trained coaches with greater credibility • Coaches would arm with the culture before but would be aware of the best practices • Would have exposure to various organization and leaders • Would be trained on various skills , tools , assessments for taking a broader view • Would be doing as a profession • Would be ensuring clients growth without any bias or pre-conceived notions • Confidentiality would be the essence • Follow up for sessions till the contract period is done with a executive summary report • Coachee opens up 100% • Would be chargeable

Engaging and Initiation

Most of the engagements can be started with generating enough insights and awareness with the coach-coachee relationship, which is the most important of all stakeholders during the assignment. The coachee could be not in a mindset always until the start and initial discussions give him/her insights to think and ask more. Few questions which can be started:

- What is the biggest transformation you would like to make in your life and career?
- What would be your top priorities which you would like to address if you hire me as a coach?
- What are your inhibitions to discuss?
- What does achievement mean to you at this juncture?
- What are the challenges which you want to overcome now?
- How important is this achievement in your life?

While as a coaching discussion, there are many questions which can engage and initiate, few of these always opens up interest and coachee starts taking the discussion with his best seriousness . Life coaching assignments which are directly discussed, normally has a high degree of active seriousness from beginning.

(Types and Effective Questions and detailed understanding would be briefed with subsequent chapters)

Benefits of having a coach: -

1. Understanding your current challenges and opportunities with more detailed insights and sub-insights.
2. Take proactive action which are smarter and planned in advance with definitive time lines
3. You can fall back on discussion of actions which are resulting to success and some actions which aren't so.
4. You have complete trust and confidentiality in place, within the organization, family etc. You open up without any biased thoughts.
5. You spend your qualitative time for yourself constructively and almost 1 hour in each session. You are the master of yourself.
6. Actions taken are faster and you feel happier, confident
7. Focused and aware of all pros and cons
8. Chances of committing errors are much reduced
9. Sustainable energy flows in you, your surroundings and contacts
10. A coach is a friend for life – who has no motive other than your success

Coaching Tool – 2. Can I coach?

How do anyone know whether I can coach others, please try this assessment?

Coaching questions for myself before I coach others	**Scale of 1-10**
I know how people behave or react to situations	1-10
I love knowing people and I enjoy their association	1-10
I am a great listener	1-10
My colleagues, friends come to me for advice	1-10
I have reflected enough on my own discovery	1-10
I understand people and their emotions, sentiments	1-10
I can gauge the depth of various situations around me	1-10
I can keep secrets	1-10
I have done enough training and coaching hours for self-grooming	1-10
I remain attached to family and friends, those who approached me for advice and help	1-10
Total – (Full Marks -100)	

Analysis for scoring:

Total Marks: 100

Scores above 90 reflects on how anyone can be a good coach, 80-90 reflects on spending more time in coaching practices, below 80 should focus on coaching skills and knowledge along with coaching practice.

Possible objections and inhibitions:

Many discussions also start with few inhibitions and objections as coaching hasn't been across all industries and processes and hasn't been actively used across human resource potential in organization.

Question: 'I do not have much time for a coaching engagement'

Possible answers:

What makes you that busy?
Are you sure about your goal planning?
How is your health with the busy schedule?
Can we spend 30 days getting ahead of your busy schedule?

Question: 'I am not sure; you can help me as a coach'

Possible answers:

Really, how do you infer this?
Is the problem overwhelming?
What are specific things you feel coach can't help u resolve?
How about working with a coach first time, a friend for life?

Question: 'I have a mentor and friend already who advices me always'

Possible answers:

Does that effectively help you plan your goals at personal and professional journey?
Is it a friendly chat or his knowledge and experience share?
What do you focus on in the conversation?
What are the areas which you feel you need strategic support?

Igniting your coaching instincts:

Although you will be seeing abundant advices and guides on how you really ignite self and coach others or become a great professional coach by simply understanding few things and prepare self.

These guidelines should give you enough clarity to begin with and lay emphasis on, how do I prepare myself before getting on the conversation.

- ✓ **My clients are complete and whole:** The most important start to know that I am privileged to have you as my coachee . All of you are growing and doing wonderful in your life, I am assisting you to expedite your personal, professional, spiritual journey mindfully. I do take you as a human being with immense talents and power, and I am sure you will discover your goals and the paths to reach it.

- ✓ **As a coach, I also do expect your active mindshare**: All conversation are planned and done with an expectation coachee with be active with his mindshare, contribute, think, plan-replan , unlearn and relearn if required , ensure coach is present and drives the relationship for his/her growth.

- ✓ **I may challenge and question on fundamentals and give straight advice:** I will be honest to drive the discussion, I will be challenging you on your thoughts to ensure there are no errors and would be clear if certain conclusions aren't sure.

- ✓ **You can use me not depend on me:** coaching starts resulting when the coachee slowly starts seeing the results and its coach's call to slowly dissociate and let coachee go independently. Coach may not fix a problem but will discuss with you and let you decide the best, coach is a resource but may not be forever. Its coachee's call during the period to ignite enough awareness to see a visible path.

- ✓ I may step back on things, look at a larger picture and discover our a probable picture look like , how perfect it would be

- ✓ I may very obvious and ask silly questions, some may be confidential with permission

- ✓ I will push for actions, I will push for a time line

- ✓ I will look towards what next steps may be important

Coaching Tool – 3. Coachability Index

To test if coachee is ready for coaching, many a times we try with **coachability index**. It's a simple tool to test the readiness, willingness for his/her need to coach

Sl.no.		**Rate yourself on 1(Low) – 5(High)**				
a	I am ready for starting on a change for self	1	2	3	4	5
b	I am OK to start actively engaging on coaching discussion	1	2	3	4	5

c	I will be honest in the discussions for my own benefit	1	2	3	4	5
d	I will park some of my rigid beliefs and try something new with coach if that's going to help me	1	2	3	4	5
e	I will start doing and working on the actions and start implementing them	1	2	3	4	5
f	If its felt, I am not getting what I wanted , I will be open to discuss and relook at my goals	1	2	3	4	5
g	I see coaching is worth an investment for my life , even if my company arranges for it	1	2	3	4	5
h	I can share my success, failures, pains and deep hidden goals and challenges	1	2	3	4	5
i	I will be ready to drive it, be ready for calls and appointments	1	2	3	4	5
j	I am ready for my current situation and would give up blaming others	1	2	3	4	5
	TOTAL					

Analysis for scoring:

Total Marks: 50

10-20: Not ready for a coaching assignment

20-30: Coachable but may break the complete cycle

30-50: Coachable, start with it.

What should be looked at in summary:

Is there an attitude to look inwards?

Is he/she willing to challenge own thought process?

Is he/she open to feedback and look into it deeply?

Is he/she demonstrating to learn, take new targets and work on them?

Am I ready for being Coached:

Its very important to assess the need. While many Coaches across the world have spoken on the subject and given several perspectives, here I would express views which should be looked by the coachee themselves. While Coach would conduct some assessments and pre-discussion for better understanding, its strongly advised to look at these inner responses and understand the responses.

- I accept my current status and look to improve/better it in future. I may not be agreeing the current status but the reality is in front of me.
- I agree to the feedback in me from my HR/Business and need to see how do I better it

- I don't agree with the goal sets shown, I have my personal goals and aspiration
- I am open to feedbacks and look at how I can guide my growth
- I look forward to be more successful in career, financially better
- I look forward to know, how I can use my potentials and talents
- I would like to see myself more ready for future challenges
- I need to be more mentally strong
- I need to inspire others
- I look forward for my own newer version of life.

Coaching Tool – 4.

My Coaching Requirement

How do I know on my coaching requirement?

1. **What is the purpose of my life?**

   ____
   ____
   ____
   ____

2. **What are my personal and professional goals?**

   ____
   ____
   ____
   ____

3. **What are my immediate concerns which I am looking ahead for solutions?**

   ____
   ____
   ____

4. **What are my strengths?**

    ____
    ____
    ____

5. **What are the areas which I feel I need to improve on?**

    ____
    ____
    ____

6. **What are my current challenges which hinders my growth?**

    ____
    ____
    ____

Few of the above questions takes you to find your purpose, values and your core objectives. It also opens up your need to get coached on certain strengths to reinforce them or some areas which you need to overcome as an area of concern, which would eventually help you achieve success in your endeavors.

Coaching GAP - Analysis:

What is GAP analysis during Coaching: GAP is the difference between what a coachee assumes his/her certain level at and what he/she would desire to be at . GAP can be for any human for any subject , here it refers to the subject which coachee desires to address on the priority . Coaching reflects on the 'NOW' status the desired status is 'THEN' .

Who defines GAP? Very important to understand that GAP is defined by a person on his/her perspective vs his/her external environment, society , personal or work life environment , value systems , beliefs , up-bringing and can continuously influence the

NOW and THEN status . Every person would have separate parameters of the checks and can define the status differently. For an individual knowing what is the current status and the desired status may not have much gaps , whereas for other individual , it can have a different desired status and hence the GAP would be higher .

Coaching awareness concentrates hugely on bringing the awareness and knowing the current and the desired status.

‘I am OK with my job and I am happy’

‘I am OK with my job and I am happy but I wanted to do something different’

‘I wanted to always do something different, I am not OK with my current status’

Please mark the 3 sentences, the statements reflect 3 different statuses. While the first reflects the parameters of being happy with the current status and the desire is not high. The second statement shows the status as good , yet there is a hidden desire , some goal is envisaged but not known . The third completely shows status which needs to be addressed on urgent basis as he/she isn’t OK with the current status.

We do not know the happiness index

We do not know the expectation index

We do not know what do you mean by OK or not OK.

Coaching addresses these in details and makes the GAP exactly clear and drives the journey for the desired state.

Let us take an example :

'I am looking out for a new job , I am not OK with my current one'

Coaching Tool – 5. GAP Analysis

What is my current job?	What do I feel is not OK?	What is my expectation?	What are my skills which I have and I want to excel on that?

On a scale of 1-10 I would rate my current skills?	What are the new skills I would like to add/improve on?	What are the other gaps I feel I have which I need to work on?	What will I do now to bridge the gap? What would be my actions now?

Clarity of certain extent will come once few of the above questions are answered and a thought process is driven on knowing the gaps and the expectation.

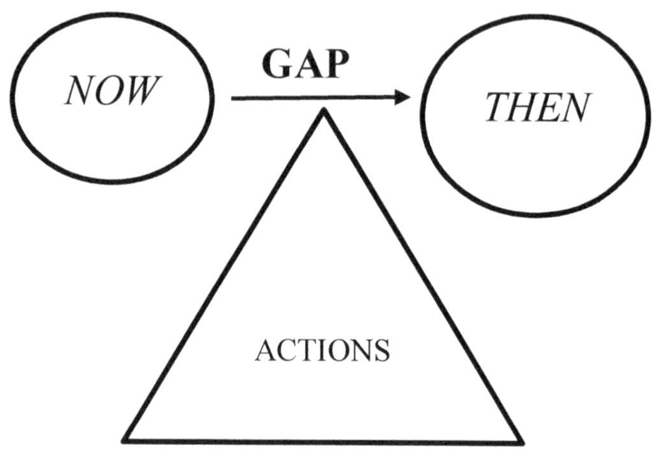

How to know what is required for me for Coaching : 'Wheel of Life'

Any individual would be having several dimensions in his/her life . 'Wheel of Life' originally created by Paul. J. Meyer , gives huge clarity to status of each concern . It's a simple visual representation of the current status of an individual and where he/she would like to see it as an aspirational status.

An individual would be broadly be having these faces :

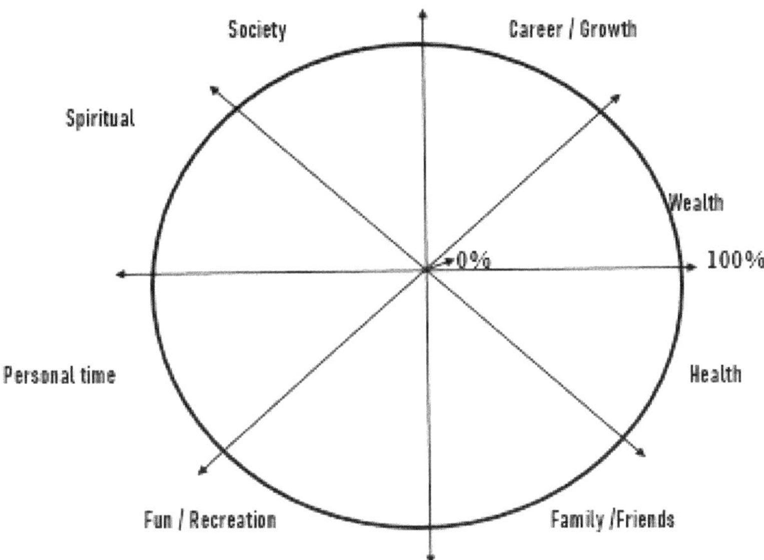

To elaborate the above circle , imagine the outer dimension of the circle to be most of the common concern of any individual like

I.	Career and Growth	V.	Fun and recreation
II.	Wealth and Finances	VI.	Personal time , space for self
III.	Health and Fitness	VII.	Spiritual
IV.	Family and Friends	VIII.	Society

Let the center of the circle be at 0% and thereafter a 10% increment at intermediate small steps with growth to touch the outer circumference. The lines from center to outer circle are spokes and the inner space is the web. The 8 parameters can be changed with more specific and detailed sub points. In a coaching conversation, these can be discussed in length.

Imagine now you start scoring 0%-100% in each above parameter on the status of current self-assessment. For example, I have not been doing well in health owing to my work. Work wise I am good and several next dreams but surely health wise I am not happy at all. Ideally in this case, career wise you may rate yourself 50% or 60% and would like to be at 90% or 100%, but clearly health wise you may be at 20% or 30%. All ratings are relative to individual and doesn't have any referral point. After drawing the 8 lines, view the circle, with a 'bird's eye view'. Longer spikes speak of your balanced wheel, combination of shorter or few longer spikes show an abnormal wheel. Shorter ones are the most concerned ones.

This tool can be a pre-assessment and start to focus on what I need coaching for, often an induvial who directly contracts for coaching is looking at what I should now concentrate more to have a better growing life .

On a executive coaching or life coaching scenario , each quadrant can have multiple spikes within and can have more specific areas to address , like within health and fitness , I may be more need to discuss , mental health , physical fitness , work-life balance , stress etc. Advised strongly to be practiced at initial stages to gauge status and pin pointing detailed addressable subjects .

Coaching Tool – 6. My Wheel of Life

Please plot your top 8 wheels as per your choice of priority (like health, finance, career etc.). Plot on scale of (0-10) / (0-100%), scale can be your choice as well. Now connect the dots from 1-8 quadrants. You have your answers of what to first solve on priority which is very important to you.

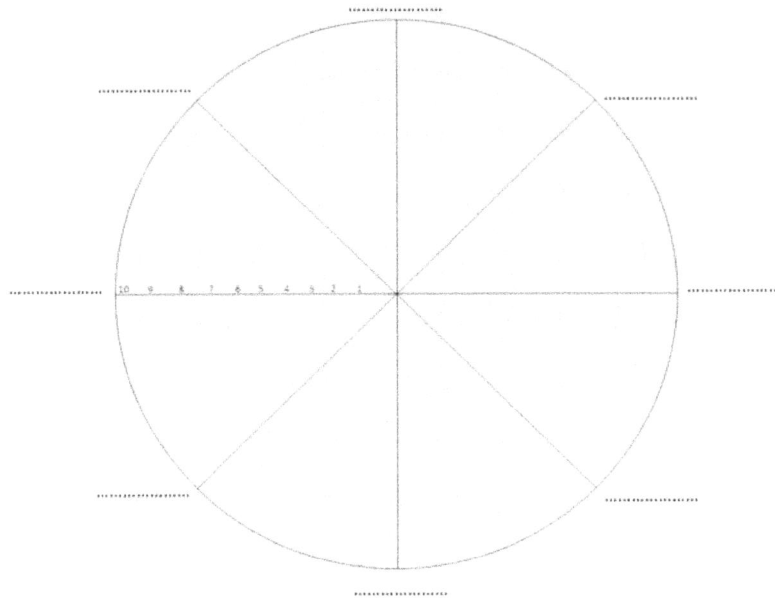

What are the active ingredients while Coaching?

Reference to the findings put by Sandra L. Davis and D. Douglas McKenna noted psychologist mentioned in their research papers along with Assay and Lambert, Bergin and Lambert. Coaching covers a sea of psychological waves or psychotherapy. Psychologists have been studying the systemic variance and how an individual responds to various orientation, assessments, techniques, programs. According to them these are the percentages of outcome which are the key elements for improvement.

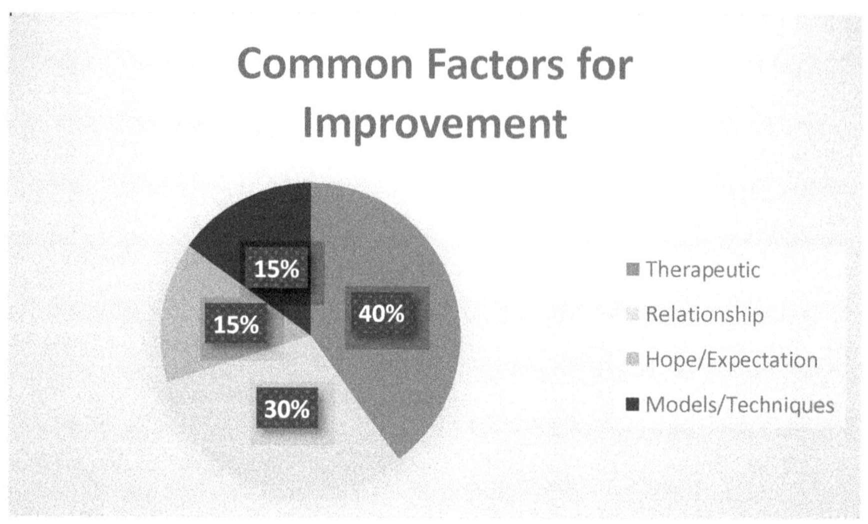

1. It's quite evident from the research that client would be bringing in about 40% his/her extra-therapeutic factors. These factors are the background of his/her knowledge, qualifications, experience, life teachings, strengths and wins, inhibitions and mentalization. It's important for the Coach to plan, practice, acknowledge the strengths and take through the process

2. 30% which is the second major chunk is the relationship, trust and bond which is created with confidence and confidentiality. Coach and Coachee finds the realistic goals and travel the process. It's an amazing twining of chords where coachee actions on discussions even when coach isn't there.

3. The next 15% is the hope, expectation and a placebo effect. Placebo is an expected effect which is felt real but may not be real. The expectation of one's change towards the goals also sets in a psychological effect within coachee for a result which is positive.

4. The next 15% refers to the models/techniques which can be always referred and can continuously emerge and change with situations .

Pie Chart above reflects on what the psychometrics, which any human would be looking at when being coached for improvements and change.

What needs to be coached for all individuals:

Coaching funnel is a methodology of the coaching flow. While evoking awareness and going by the top core areas of improvement, many have asked me as to what we address while coaching and since coaching is effective, what gets corrected for all which gives such better results.

Here I would refer to my coach Mr. John Mattone and his references to **'Intelligent Leadership Wheel'.**

Intelligent Leadership Wheel is a clear focus of knowing human behavior which we see and what we do not see. Clearly, they are categorized under 'Inner-Core' and the 'Outer-Core'.

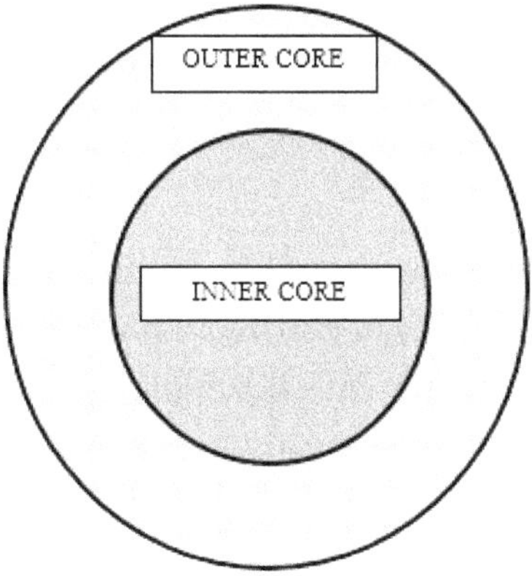

The Wheel of Intelligent Leadership by John Mattone

Inner Core:

To know the actual leader and the true person, the inner core needs to be understood. Any person is inside out and not outside in. What does that mean? What comprises it? The inside core is your character and the constituent of that character which is deep engraved in yourself. Character is the core of human being and is formed by

- Values
- Beliefs
- References

Values are those elements of life which is the most important aspect. It lies deep within which defines what is wrong and what is right and picks which is good for us , desirable and should be worth . Values drive your subsequent decision between what can be good or otherwise. Beliefs are derived from every source since childhood and forms certain concepts which makes a logical decision within subconsciously accepting something which is true or false. Human minds have some beliefs which can be through education, culture, religion, society and keep influencing one. Some beliefs may not be true or correct to others but can be true to the individual and that cannot be normally seen or understood. References are parameters of understanding of values and beliefs which can be unique to each. Honesty, loyalty, courage, modesty, diligence form the inner core.

Values and beliefs create thoughts, behavior and emotions form the outer layer of your inner core. Thoughts can be positive or negative. Emotions can be varied which can be reactive, proactive or flat. Behavior is when thoughts and emotions reflect outside. This is the first outlook which is seen outside of an individual.

Therefore any behavior which is seen other than you, would be a resultant of several layers of values , beliefs and their reactive impetus thoughts and emotions , hence when you see anyone with a behavior which may be termed as good or bad is an outcome of properties lying deeper than you see .

Coaching addresses this deep inner core to slowly see the change in behavior.

Outer Core:

Having understood the inner core and the constituents, outer core is easier to understand. Outer core elements which form from the inner core are:

- Critical thinking
- Decision making
- Strategic thinking
- Emotional leadership
- Communication skills
- Talent leadership
- Team leadership
- Change leadership
- Drive for results

The outer core elements are pure manifestations of the inner core and gets driven by the inner core. Outer core competencies are gauged with various assessment parameters and be understood for what is the level of the current status and expected status.

How can the inner core be strengthened? Internal beliefs and values can be strengthened to form a mindset which leverages your strengths and works on the gaps. Power of will, thinking holistically, tuning for correctness and ability to be present on the current status and being vigilant can better your inner core. Coaching process takes through the steps for realization and correctives.

How can the outer core be strengthened? Each of the above outer core competency can be mapped and taken through a series of detailed assessments for current status and various training and coaching interventions for correctives of outer core.

Individual who would look for a lasting change on the outer core need to necessarily address the inner core for seeing the change which is sustained and effective for all situations thereafter.

The Coaching Funnel

Coaching funnel has been explained by Icon Border in Performance Strategies. It follows a funnel with some flow charts to give it more logic and clarity. All the fundamental process gets completed with ICF core competencies and adherence to the funnel and flowchart leads to the best results expected.

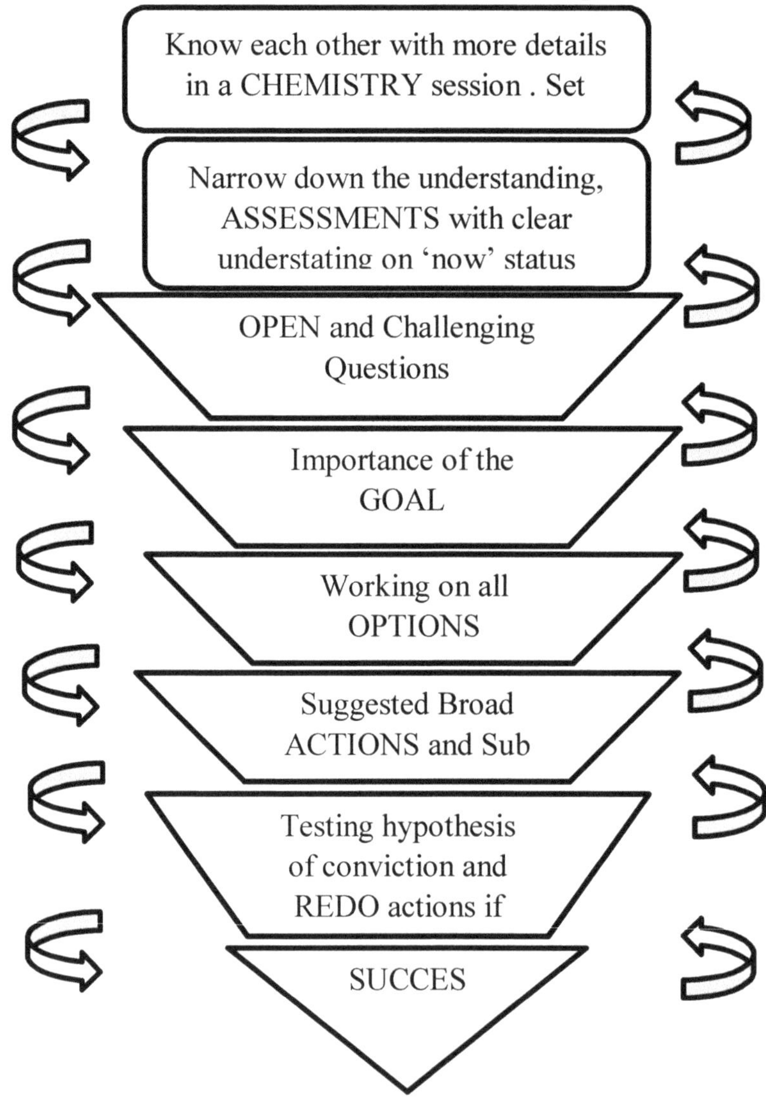

1. The flow and the funnel start with a ‘Chemistry’ session which is as mentioned earlier, forms a clear understanding of the Coachee, his/her views and opinion. Discussion of each coaching outcome and aligning the relation to the objective which can be sharper with due course of discussion.

2. All assessments and formative ideas to support the objectives may be important. Many a times new assessments and exercises may be carried out with the objectives in mind to have clarity on the status. It’s important that Coach and Coachee are aligned to the NOW status. It’s a reality check or a foundation management.

3. The actual conversation can be through series of conversation with more open-ended questions. Sometimes the answers or status needs to be questioned with more challenging, probing, leading questions and give a deeper search to answers, these stages have a huge discovery process.

4. The discussion gradually led to GOAL, forming a goal and ensuring it’s the right goal needs more deeper understanding. Importance of the GOAL in the coachee’s life or the need of the coachee’s contribution in an organization would be essential to know. Many a times coachee’s goal and organization’s goal may differ, whereas in direct coaching contracts it may be not the issue.

5. Options and all the possible solutions is what the conversation can dwell with and find the best solution which can work for him/her. This is the time when the coachee realizes his/her strength and works out what would be the best options and solution in mind.

6. Thereafter the phase of active actions starts with coachee implementing actions. This phase is the real test of putting your thoughts in action. It's a transformation of self, many actions are intangible, psychological, emotional and behavioral, hence they would be slow. Many of the actions may be broad and need micro or sub actions below it and hence needs to be carefully drafted and reviewed.

7. Testing your own conviction and hypothesis – This is very critical for your own analysis which need conviction and testing while you are implementing the actions. Some actions which are assumed to be working, may not be actually working for results. The check of the thoughts, estimating probable loopholes and working towards closing them.

8. Success of achievement. Here as a coach, I have been harping on my coaching lectures to applaud each intermediate success milestone . Small milestones seek better appreciations and acknowledgements. Larger goals are better reached comfortably.

9. Now each step has a loop back and back again. Now it reflects as a reverse flowchart for going back every step, when the advance step is not resulting a forward direction. For example – A goal step arrived after due deliberations of questions, asking and thoughts may go back again to the same stage if coachee feels the goal may be not correct or it needs to be clearer and more specific etc. Hence each process should be taken due time and should be moved in the same sequence.

"Survival strategy for modern fittest – Learn, Unlearn, Relearn"

THE THREADS OF COACHING

Chapter - 3

Coaching is a seamless flow of events and it's like one bead to the next while making a beautiful garland. Coaching is so intriguing that people often get confused as why it needs to be learnt. A certified coach knows the finer points of understanding and the preparations it needs to do as a coach before any conversation.

Quite beautifully explained by ICF in its guidelines and also by Laura Whitworth, Karen and Henry Kimsey and Philip Sandhal in Co-Active Coaching.

Imagine the following coaching scenarios;

1. Coach is young, certified 40's and coachee is a very senior CX in a huge organization and is around 50's.
2. Coach is a senior executive around 45's and coachee is an employee who may be in different department of the organization around same age, may be in lower designation, is an average performer.
3. Coachee is a housewife who is coming back after her gap in career and wanted to see how does she ensure she covers up the goals/achievements in next 5 years.
4. Coachee is a student and coach is the father

5. Coachee is father and coach is the son

What are the mind sets you can assume from the above of the coachee and what would be the mindset preparation of coach?

Apparently, in few situations coach looks at higher knowledge, experience, in some it may sound opposite.

COACHING IS AGNOSTIC TO AGE, EXPERIENCE, BACKGROUND, DOMAIN KNOWLEDGE AND ANY PREVIOUS STATUS.

Remember the previous point, its NOW TO THEN (FUTURE).

So, what does that constitute.
Every individual or coachee is

1. COMPLETE
2. RESOURCEFUL
3. TALENTED
4. GIFTED
5. CREATIVE
6. CAN FIND HIS/HER ANSWER
7. CAN DRIVE SELF
8. CAN REACH DESTINATION

This is one of the most interesting and core of coaching. A coach should be absolutely clear in his/her thoughts that my coachee exhibits all quality and it's my job to guide the process to success. To elaborate,

Coach does not fix or go in the conversation to fix and find the solution for him/her. It's the discovery process which gradually unfolds.

Coachee would most often start from a position, if he/she haven't gone through previous coaching, would not be aware of themselves. It is the coach to instill confidence, courage and thoughts in a coachee about his/her completeness. Anybody and everybody is complete on their thoughts, is enough creative, has may talents and can sail towards the destination.

It reminds again to the Indian mythology of 'The Ramayana', Lord Hanuman and his hidden potential and talents. Lord Hanuman was supremely powerful, but was cursed in his childhood that he would forget all his strengths and might, till somebody reminds him of all his strength in a needful situation. A need aroused when somebody had to cross the seas to reach Lanka. It was at that moment when Lord Hanuman was reminded of his strength, might and un-imaginary gifted talents of flying. Upon recalling he could recall his strength and could demonstrate his stupendous potential and power and play one of the most vital roles of winning over the mighty evils for which he is remembered forever. The epic can also be read in 'Hanuman Chalisa' a hym of him .

While the above may be a story, it recalls that a coach can play an active role and invoke a deep thinking to arouse one's potential till the time its recognized for the benefit of the individual. We are limited to average mindsets, limiting beliefs, past experiences and undermine self. What gets later drafted in ICF manuscripts, is something which can be taken as a learning coincidence from the above. All humans have amazing thoughts and learnings, which needs better and clear understanding. Any coaching scenario takes this as a fundamental and concrete pre-understanding or else the entire conversation is judgmental and biased.

A coach is a friend for Life: When I first heard this, I found it to be simple or may be just a proverb used to hype the emotional connect. Then once I started getting coached, I realized the true essence of the short quote. You are not the boss, senior, parent, teacher, junior, low or high etc. You are a friend of the coachee first and lay the foundation with a clear self-less attitude. You are forming the foundation of trust, confidentiality and a bonding where coachee can reach out for all his queries. You can arrange meetings, calls, discussion based on best availability but please ensure the relation is longer and reachable. Many coaching clients often call and would appraise you of various positive changes post assignment also, acknowledge and appreciate with a friendly atmosphere. It propels the coachee's growth to amazing heights.

Evoking awareness:

Imagine yourself as a coachee and think of the situations:

1. I know I can't raise my voice; I miss speaking up at the moment
2. I am good at presenting, but often fumble when doing so in front of my seniors or boss
3. You know at home I am quite different, don't know what happens here
4. I am good with my friend, I can't talk about his bad habits
5. I have been always performing, the new management is sure to notice
6. My confidence mellows during public speaking
7. Despite my best efforts, I miss deadlines
8. I know walking is good, still I feel lazy in mornings
9. Smoking isn't good, trying to leave it last few years, could not do so
10. I wanted to do this always, I could not get time for it

The situations above and many more would be common across. What we speak and assume is our current status and we assume it to be like that.

It's the coach's responsibility to dissect the current status of the coachee and understand the real status behind. Coach may ask you:

- curious questions
- questions challenging your beliefs
- asking you on certain assumptions, which you may already believed it
- describe your goals, plans quite in details
- recall certain strengths which you may have or would have displayed previously or as simple as a most memorable event which makes you feel proud about yourself
- how did you manage such tasks earlier, what pushed you, what do you appreciate yourself on that?
- draw an analogy or build a futuristic journaling for asking what you could have done more, better or stronger
- may ask you to draw your future
- may take you through some activities, assessments
- maximize your options
- hypothesis of your options, testing
- how your options aligned to goals, values

The whole process is, for making you constructively think deep, when you are questioned and asked questions, answers are thought. The beauty of coaching is when you start seeing the reality with these answers and it ALWAYS HAPPEN. Coachee sinks in his plans, identifies what's happening good and what's missing. This becomes a constructive understanding and forms a strong pillar in the journey.

For Example:

A simple status may be that 'I am doing good in my company and look for my promotion to reach the top management'

Some questions which may evoke

- What were your biggest contributions?
- How were you able to execute them?
- What do you think are the new challenges put forth now?
- What are the expectations from you nowadays?
- What are the few things you are focusing on now?
- What makes you confident enough for the promotion?
- What additional actions can be looked into?

These may be few questions , but would surely arouse many answers and if thought carefully may open many vistas of next planning your options .

LISTENING AND UNDERSTANDING

What do you mean by listening?

What is understanding?

Think and answer ……... it creates the difference!

Dictionary meaning –

Listening: **(verb) to pay attention to somebody/something that you can hear.**

Understanding**:** **(noun) the knowledge that somebody has about a particular subject or situation .**

Listening is an art which I slowly understood and tried to better the skills every day in my life. It's a process of hearing ……hearing ……. hearing actively and then actively engage.

In a conversation, there are many instances, the listener doesn't even see while somebody is talking to him/her, some miss words or feelings, some only want to listen few words which are interesting or important to them, some listen but don't gauge the depth or understand, some understand but do not react or engage, so on and so forth.

Listening is a talent which slowly gets trained in a coach. A leader or any person can shape up the skill with active hearing abilities of knowing the right approach towards it and master the art. Listening is one of the most important grooming abilities of a leader for knowing others well.

Listening opens up your coachee , or anybody whom you are talking to . The interaction starts both ways with huge active engagement and the conversation yields a way. Passive conversation is when listening is poor. Most people do not listen actively, may be their daily work doesn't make them aware of the need. Imagine you talking to a customer support executive, they would quickly take down all points which you spoke, also they record the conversation for training purpose, why? It's not only to shape their behavioral response and resolution but also to see whether the executive has correctly understood the issue and gave the right revert. Recall a conversation with your friend or spouse or boss

'I wanted to say this ……………'

'I meant this ……. while I was explaining….'

'Didn't you understand'

'Please repeat'

'Sorry, this is not what I said'

'Let me say this again'

And many more of such conversation happens.

Most of the time, we are engaged in our world, our priorities, our own baggage, our own conclusions and experience.

Our biggest mistake many a time, **we listen short, we listen wrong, we quickly draw a conclusion and we judge the person in a quick conversation.**

On the other side, we normally expect, we should be heard better. Our friends, relatives, colleagues, boss should hear us completely and they should understand us completely. I am sure we will be able to give some clarity in the coaching context.

Advantages of good listening:

- Conversation results with a positive outcome
- Improve relation
- You get better answers
- Avoid conflicts and confusion
- Resolve problems faster
- Improves you as a mature personality
- You get acknowledged
- Coachee looks to talk again

Types of Listening for effectiveness in any conversation:

1. **Listen – With Ears**
2. **Listen – With Ears, Eyes, Open Mind**
3. **Listen – With Ears, Eyes, Open Mind, Respond, Reciprocate, Engage.**

"When you talk, you only speak what you know, if you listen and listen better, you know what you don't know"

-His Holiness Dalai Lama, Buddhist Guru

"Listen to understand, not to reply immediately"

Level 1:

Imagine you have gone to a store to buy a new mobile handset, what would you like to hear? You would like to hear somebody speaks to you on price, features, offers etc., right?

This level of interaction is when someone speaks, the receiver is already tuned to his/her previous engagements, pre-occupation, own thoughts and ideas, his/her previous such instances or experience, judgments. Here the receiver is HEARING, MAY NOT be listening. The speaker may complete the discussion and receiver may have not responded or asked anything or would have already formed his/her ideas. Here you may be present but not be listening.

Level 2:

Imagine again with walking into the mobile store for the mobile handset, the executive would be handling many customers, suddenly he comes near you and sits with you and says 'sir, please tell me what exactly you require, often you note he is nodding his head, as to understand exactly to what is the requirement and also says 'yes' in between to confirm he heard. Wont it be great to ask for more and continue the discussion? 'I heard you sir, you might be requiring a handset with high storage', won't you feel better that the executive have started responding similarly to your requirements.

The level of interaction here is the speaker is saying something and the receiver is giving his 100% focus and attention. To notice, many of the conversation happens with non-verbal response. Like a direct eye-to-eye contact, nodding in affirmation, facial response, body response can be understood for ensuring the two-way communication is engrossed. You start to understand speakers voice, tonality, pitch of words, use of words. You can paraphrase the sentence and form your own simple reply with 'if I heard you well, you asked for ....' 'What I understand is that you would need......' is a great art for ensuring you are listening, responding and checking the speaker's response to the subject.

Level 3:

Imagine again with walking into the mobile store for the mobile handset, the executive says, "what you are looking, I heard you and this is a phone with your specs, but I feel you have more things to ask, please ask sir", you keep the discussion up 'yes you are right, I wanted to also know...." "I guessed so...., this handset not only helps you......but also......". Imagine your happiness.

These conversations are Level 2 + your own intuition + environment. It means when the conversation happen, speaker and listener are almost in the flow status. Apart from the emotions, sentiments, you are surrounded by environment which keeps adding with non-verbal communication of sight, feel, touch, smell and you seem to be a 'trans' where the flow isn't governed by you. At this stage coachee is almost driven by words flowing. As a coach you can take charge and drive this vibrant energy and flow towards responses which creates impact. This is the hyperactive state of interaction where the environment joins in prompting, saying, talking about things which coachee would not have otherwise spoken.

Please practice while in conversation:

- **Repeat** – you can repeat the words used by speaker, to ensure your presence and that you have been active in conversation.

- **Paraphrase** – repeat the same using the same essence and spirit with similar words.

- **Reflecting -** message retold with own words , sentence made concise.

Level 3 conversation sample:

- **Coachee:** Month end is near; I have assignments and targets all pending and short – and my promotion discussion is scheduled next week.
- **Coach:** How important is the promotion? This would be your long pending aspiration.
- **Coachee:** Yes, that's all I have been working for so long and prepared last 3 years, but also this month's targets look scary.
- **Coach:** I can sense the dream but you seem to be scared for this month target
- **Client:** Pauses...... do I hear like that?
- **Coach:** Yes, I heard you a little afraid of your promotion discussion
- **Client:** Thinks and takes a deep breath, No I don't want to look or talk like that, I need to be more prepared for that and should sound confident . I will see what best I can put forth to make the month effective.
- **Coach:** Now I see the leader back, what are you going to do to be more confident.
- **Client:** Surely, will work out with more details of my work and achievements so far, but more than that I will practice talking boldly and put forth my contributions with enough conviction.

- **Coach:** Wow, best wishes and I am sure you would do wonders.

In the above paragraph, the sequence of events, takes the discussion through Level 1, 2, 3. Coach is able to sense and listen more of his fear which may be common to the situation. Coachee would look towards few things which may dampen the larger goals for some intermediate challenges. Coach would re-instill the courage, confidence and pause. Coachee thinks, goes into a thinking mode as to whether the current challenges should bow him down from the bigger goals. Coachee comes back with more confidence that the bigger goals need different preparation and action plans and shorter objective can have different plans but will try best to justify both. Here coach listens carefully to the tone, pitch and can understand that more than the current month target issue, coachee is afraid of the promotion discussion which is not uttered in the conversation. Hence a careful, deep, active listening is an active ingredient for the coaching conversation.

Critical thinking related to listening:

Critical thinking is the process of listening deeper, analyse and synthesize the data of what you hear. It involves the need for evaluation and metacognition with high degree of qualitative screening to draw right conclusions. Paraphrasing is an excellent technique to ensure you hear without distraction, hear words and beyond it and actively repeat when required with paraphrase and check its validity before concluding.

All leaders, who frequently speak, address gathering, meetings, forums should develop critical thinking with active listening to ensure your communications are effective.

Words and phrases which coachee may speak or may not speak but could arouse awareness and introspection:

- Saying ‘No’
- Missed doing something /not responding/keeping quiet
- Words spoken and actions are contradicting
- Tone and words don’t match
- Excitement in the words
- Pause and the silence which is speaking large
- All words refer a dream within
- Very charged and motivating
- Ready with new ideas and speaks up
- Low on thinking bandwidth
- Known or unknown domain
- Paused with a breath
- Sweating on a particular thought
- Very feeble response
- Voice with remorse or pain
- Not hearing but responding fast
- Desire to do whatever is needed
- Honesty and faithful
- Too much care for people
- Priority to others much beyond than usual
- Head on attitude
- Stressed and fatigued
- Quick and responsive
- Restricted thoughts
- Crying over other’s shoulder
- Self-cry manifested

There are various situations, when you exactly do not hear the background of subject but the above illustrations are reflective on subject and background which may be spoken and as a great coach, you would be discovering these aspects of the coachee to develop on the coaching journey.

The listener has to hear beyond the words which opens several other dimensions of the actual context and is a great art of knowing what's not spoken.

Art of Questioning

What do we all mean by questioning and what is the relevance of questioning in coaching conversation?

Imagine on a level 3 coaching conversation, you are listening and understanding your coachee, you are now actively engaged and very active 'into' the session and participating with your verbal and non-verbal responses. That's when you start being interested in the conversation as you are focused in it, you are away from all distractions and glued to the discussion.

You would be curious with lot of queries; millions of thoughts would be processed in you as a coach as the coachee would be also thinking and going through several thoughts.

Humans are by nature very affectionate; they tend to help somebody when they hear something which he/she can help. As a coach you would have processed all the critical thoughts, analyzed and now you have become super curious .

What do you do now?

As a coach, the first thing is to now UNDERSTAND and STOP GIVING ANY ADVICE out of your previous knowledge, experience, similar situations, relationships. The biggest mistake is to ensure not to jump to give solutions. Instead **hold back yourself now to be curious and ask your question**.

Remember, coaching is all about evoking awareness in clients / coachee . Advices are instructions or suggestions which may be working for somebody but may not act as a standard prescription for all.

Questions evoke this awareness, which results in the coachee to think and re-think and come up with his/her own answers, analyze the answers and rethink on actions. Suggesting solutions which is primarily meant as mentoring doesn't ensure that the coachee would be thinking and finding the suggestion as a quick fix solution, which may or may not work.

Shift from the 'tell' mode to 'ask' mode.

Asking the right question, keeping it sharp, keeping it short, evoking thoughts, making the coachee talk, makes the coaching conversation to go on the right direction.

Note: in a typical conversation, coach should talk not more than 25% of the total time and the rest 75% of the time, the coachee need to talk. This is where the coachee is thinking and finding its own solution.

"Ask the right questions if you going to find the right answers"

– Venessa Redgrave

How does right questions help the conversation?

- You have empowered the coachee to think
- Coachee is planning his/her own actions
- Coachee takes control of the situation
- Coachee finding answers, has better commitment
- Coachee is all powerful and coach is a guide
- Amazing emotional bonds created as coachee speaks from heart
- Conversation helps coachee become more confident
- 'If and but', options are driven by coachee

Therefore, asking questions is now like mastering the art of asking the right questions. It takes years to master this craft as a coach and I am sure the book would help many improve on their awareness and conversation post reading. It's an art which arouses mind to be more creative, affirmative and productive.

Questions which are open ended, questions which are powerful and thought provoking, questions which make you think are to be practiced not only for being a coach, but also for your regular conversation.

TONALITY, PITCH, AND NON-VERBAL GESTURES:

To ensure you are on the process of mastering asking questions, tone and pitch of your voice does matter a lot. Tone is how your voice sounds when you say a particular thing. Tonality moderation, pitch of voice, body gestures does makes around 80% impact to the overall communication which was meant. Words and content make only around 10-20%. Pitch is acoustic co-relation or the auditory emphasize of words depending on the situation, it can be low or high. It plays a vital role in the communication and one should practice.

For Ex:

"Come here", a superior's tone may be different to a friend's

EFFECT OF TONALITY , NON VERBAL GESTURES AND WORDS IN CONVERSATION

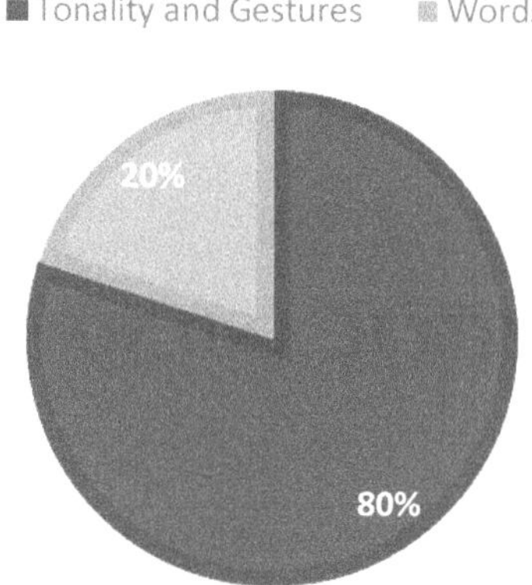

Hearing a particular incident, you may react 'wow'. When you react for something, you are expecting, it can be expressed softly but when you hear something unexpected, it can be a large 'wow'. Here the pitch changes and the expression are different with different emphasis.

Asking questions also make a huge difference when tone and pitch is taken care while asking or having a simple conversation.

Non-verbal gestures are the body signs and signals made during the conversation, are your body gestures responding to the answers, admittance, experience or queries. That makes a huge impact and counts higher than just what the content of your speaking.

So what questions are asked, what can be practiced and what to be avoided?

USE: OPEN – ENDED QUESTIONS,

WHICH ENSURES MAXIMUM OUTCOME

Types of questions:

Questions can be of various types, here's a quick reference:

- ✓ **Open Questions** – These are best types and to be used widely in any conversation. Open questions mostly start with 'What', can be also with 'Who' or 'How' or 'Where' but use of 'What' is most prevalent and gives very powerful meaning of the question. Also it propels the coachee for thinking and he/she starts replying with deeper insights.

Examples:

1. What is your goal?
2. What makes you happy?
3. What can ensure you do better this time?
4. What are your strengths?
5. What is the purpose of your life?
6. What makes you sure about taking this step?
7. What may go wrong now?
8. How would you describe your experience?
9. Who can be a better coach than you yourself?
10. Where do you find happiness?

Most of the above answers would start making the coachee answer 1-2 sentences or more and makes the conversation interesting and forward looking.

(Most questions can be converted to 'What' questions …. Try !!)

How the essence changes?

Example: Conversation between Manager to Executive

Case -I

Manager - 'Why have you not done this work?'

Executive – 'Yes……Oh…. I wanted to say…. but you know…'

Case – II

Manager – 'What is the reason behind non-completion of this work?'

Executive – 'Yes I tried …but could complete only 80%, expect to complete today'

Shaping of the same situation and question, can change altogether the expected reply. Case -II opens with a 'what' question, which necessarily opens the conversation, conversation is not sudden bounded and the speaker gets a much better reply which can be further dwelled on. Case -I is pushing the coachee into a shell and discussion is incomplete with manager not getting a complete reply.

- ✓ **Clarifying questions, Explanatory Questions** – It's a continuation of the open questions with going to the next stage of going further on the conversation. Explanations and clarifying can help coachee go further to explain the same with more details, clarify the position. Here the explanation and clarifications help the coachee be more speaking about his/her answer and feels complete that his/her point was well explained and clarified.

Examples:

1. Tell me more about ….?
2. What are the various goals you are now pursuing?
3. Can you clarify your point of …...?
4. Can you explain, what does happiness mean to you?
5. Which options do you feel, you should work on?
6. It sounds interesting, may I ask you to speak more on ….

- ✓ **Scaling questions –** This is to directly assess the current status and projected plans. Any situation and status can be directly concluded with a suggested status. Scale can be any as per the requirement, mostly scale of 1-10 is preferred. Coach can quickly guess the status of condition, preparedness, progress and sharpness on current levels. It is also used to put a suggested level, target expectation of the next goal.

Examples:

1. On a scale of 1-10, how sure are you for meeting your targets this month?
2. How would you like to rate yourself on a scale of 1-5, on your plans?
3. With respect to your actions so far, how sure are you on a scale of 1-10?
4. If you are now on 5 on a scale of 1-10, what would you target in next 3 months on same scale?
5. Please map the success chances on the scale of 1-10?

- ✓ **Reflective questions** – It's a reflection of the coachee regarding any situation for introspection. It provokes for a moment where there may be a temporary pause or silence post asking, when coachee thinks and analyses.

Examples:

1. What was your learning out of this incident?
2. What does success look like to you now...?
3. How does this belief form your actions?
4. What can be done to stop repeat such occurrence in future?
5. Pause and reflect, what could you have done better?

- ✓ **Situational / Hypothetical** – It takes the discussion to a level which may be hypothetical in nature. For a moment coachee can be taken on a status which may be imaginary, hypothetical and an artificial situation.

Examples:

1. Imagine, you had taken the position of __, what would be your actions to get the best answer?
2. Had you achieved the trophy, how would life look like to you?
3. If you had to shift the roles, what would have been your first priority?
4. What would you do if an angry customer confronts you?
5. How would life look when you would have done the work?

✓ **Result Centric** – Often conversations get drawn back by negative emotions, expected failures, previous experiences and tends to be not looking forward. In such situations the path becomes the focus not the result. Conversations which can lead us to result and outcome can be the focus areas. Such questions are always forward looking, addresses your strengths, your positive core competencies and a situation emerges where possibilities of achievements are looked higher.

Examples:

1. Understand you had many opportunities earlier, what did you focus on to win?
2. What an achievement! what steps did you take to ensure similar urgencies ensure better results henceforth?
3. Which are the changes you can now do, to see it as the best you?
4. How did you the manage the crisis with such good results?
5. What top priorities can be handled now for maximum benefit?

There can be variety of many other questions which can be asked like paradoxical, motivational, spiritual, value based etc., with the above-mentioned types, most questions can be covered in coaching conversation for results.

So, what does questions do to human mind?

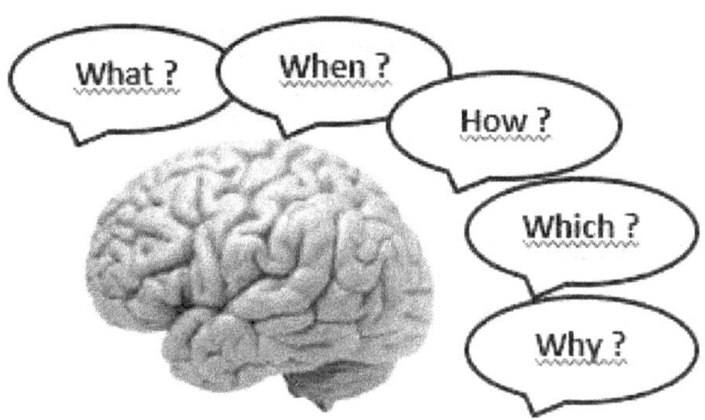

Brain has been a complex cellular structure of neurons. When a question is asked, there is a rush of serotine (hormone released by brain in reaction to various moods and feelings). There is an instant reflex called as "instinctive elaboration", which makes the brain think about the answer.

Researchers in neuroscience elaborate that brain can function to think about one idea at a time. Neuroscientist John Medina in his book *Brain Rules*, say we can't multitask, even if we are asked to or assume to do so. The more challenging questions arouse the brain to think more and leave out many other thoughts which may be playing at the back.

Neuroplasticity is the flexibility of the neurons which change locations to the response to questions and goes creative with new learning and good questions provoke it.

Some questions which help:

- At the end of an answer, 'what else?' provokes more answers
- Assume you are aware 'what would have been your answer?'
- 'What can be advantage or disadvantage you see here?'
- 'What do you lose doing it?'
- 'What do you gain doing it?'

- ‘Where does this head to?’
- ‘If not now, when?’
- ‘What’s running in your mind now?’
- ‘What can be one learning out of it?’
- ‘In such a situation, what’s your best advice?’
- ‘What’s new can you think ahead?’
- ‘What more?’
- ‘Is that Ok or you can do more?’

Coaching tool – 7.

What are your best questions?

Try to re-ask with open ended questions.

(Convert your asks to open with what, which, when…)

____

____

____

____

____

Cartesian Questioning method:

This technique of questioning is a great tool on how a particular decision can be made on a question. Decision making process with a question would be critical for the continuation of the coaching process and this tool can be useful. Formulated by Rene Descartes, a French philosopher and mathematician before 1650. Cartesian plane would be popular in mathematics where it hints at a point being mapped to a either a X axis or a Y axis on a plane.

Cartesian questioning has 4 quadrants which can be used for any question

- WHAT WILL HAPPEN IF I DO?
- WHAT WON'T HAPPEN IF I DO?
- WHAT WILL HAPPEN IF I DON'T?
- WHAT WON'T HAPPEN IF I DON'T?

	WILL	WON'T
DO	WHAT WILL HAPPEN IF I DO?	WHAT WON'T HAPPEN IF I DO?
DON'T	WHAT WILL HAPPEN IF I DON'T	WHAT WON'T HAPPEN IF I DON'T?

So how do we practice in coaching? All question can be grouped into the 4 quadrants and can be looked at with insights for a suitable understanding and a way forward. My analysis has been to these quadrants as :

	WILL	WON'T
DO	POSITIVE OUTLOOK	ASSUMED NEGATIVE
DON'T	ASSUMED POSITIVE	NEGATIVE OUTLOOK

Let's understand with an example:

'I want to start a new business'

	WILL	WON'T
DO	WHAT WILL HAPPEN IF I DO? • I have a new profession • I have a new source of earning • I can be an entrepreneur as I always wanted to	WHAT WON'T HAPPEN IF I DO? • I may not earn more • I will not be pursuing my goals • I will not become an entrepreneur
DON'T	WHAT WILL HAPPEN IF I DON'T • I continue with my job • I remain happy with what I am doing • I will remain dissatisfied	WHAT WON'T HAPPEN IF I DON'T? • I stop my growth • I will remain wanting • I lose my own will

You can shape up any questions thereafter on the above quadrants and arrive at which quadrant makes your 1st choice on a subject.

Coaching Tool – 8.

You can try this on your possessions:

What are the things which I want, which I already have?

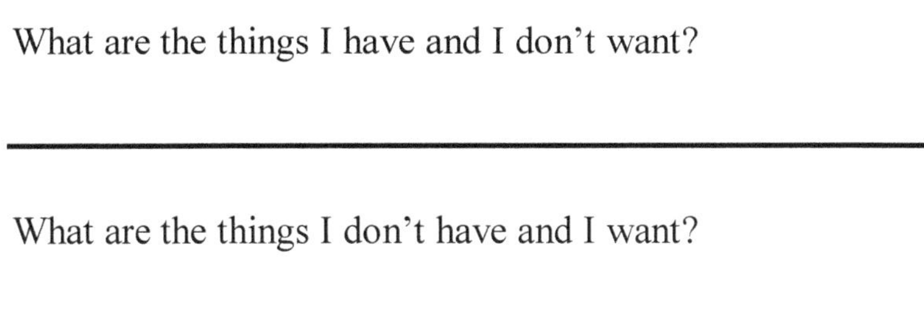

What are the things I have and I don't want?

What are the things I don't have and I want?

What are the things I don't have and I don't want?

Polarity Mapping:

Coaching opens up with detailed understanding of how any situation can have both positives and negatives or sometimes both are equally important and we need to strike a balance. Coaching opens the big picture and coachee understands the paradoxes are opportunities for transformation.

- Should we inhale or exhale?
- Should a company plan consolidation or growth?
- Should we focus on innovation or sustenance?
- Do I look for short term or long-term plans now?

Problems give ideas which may be opposed or are conflicting. Polarities on the other hand are complimenting ideas and are interdependent. These does not need a decision to be in which side but needs balancing. Often there can be hundreds of queries in coachee's mind and each one of them would be complimenting and would not be dipoles. Hence polarity mapping and coaching on polarity is focused on understanding the fine balance one needs to achieve at certain aspects to have greater clarity and forward approach.

For Example: Breathing is not a choice between inhaling and exhaling. It's a fine balance between the two which leads to have a great breathing.

'I want to excel in career but I am not mobile'

'I would like to start business but not ready yet to quit my job'

It's a question between 'OR' and 'AND'

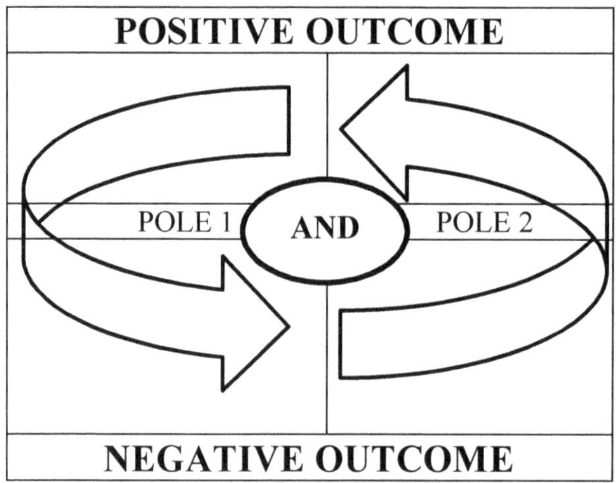

- Balance between confident and being humble
- Balance between showing authority and collaboration
- Balance between freedom and responsibility
- Balance between super success and super failure
- Balance between leading and empowering

What to avoid during asking questions?

Any coaching conversation can have multiple snags of flow and can disrupt the conversation. Certain type of questions doesn't arouse the conversation which is desired structurally with the objective. What can be the disruptors?

a) **Why question:** Human psychology avoids being probed or scrutinized during any conversation. References of probing always digs into the past occurrences and makes the coachee think back. If the occurrence would have been with a fond result it may lead to long explanation of attributes and personal brag. In case of the occurrence not resulting in a positive result, it may be a reminiscence of unhealthy or poor memories. It may push for reasons beyond an explanation or unnecessary be duplicitous.

   Imagine a worker could not complete a task, a supervisor would ask 'Why have you not completed the work?' Now the worker would have many reasons and explanations, often he would say with a frozen tone and in a composed fashion. Supervisor would still have not got the reply.

   Largely 'why' questions make the coachee/client/listener composed and go into shell and may come with limited or improper answers. These questions should be avoided in the conversation.

b) **Successive questions:** Questions can be asked one after the other and confuses the coachee on which one to address first, also he/she may forget the next question while explaining the first. Confusion is ought to happen and too many answers clog the mind to put forth the right and best answer. Such questions are to be avoided completely.

   What made you fail and why haven't you taken care?
   Why do you talk so much about it and how does that impact our results?

c) **Leading questions:** Coach can be aware of certain facts and outcome. It may be moving towards a question, the answer of it would be quite certain or obvious based on general or known outcome. This does not allow the coachee to think beyond the situation and may obviously provide the same expected answer. While this may be useful for the conversation with some quick positive outcome, the client's awareness may not be seen genuinely. These may also reflect on assumptions, interlinked statements, implications or intimidations.

Will exercises in the morning not be useful for you?
Do you prefer overtime since your earnings have fallen?
You seem to be a happy customer, aren't you?

d) **Explaining and briefing the question already asked:** It is often used in common conversation where questions are often complicated and needs explanation of the same. Such questions often are not understood, not clear and are confused. It again confuses coachee to think and think too many things.

Don't you feel agonized? I wanted to say don't you feel frustrated, worried? I hope you are understanding!

Why are you feeling guilty, what's the point of feeling bad now, do you need to feel anxious?

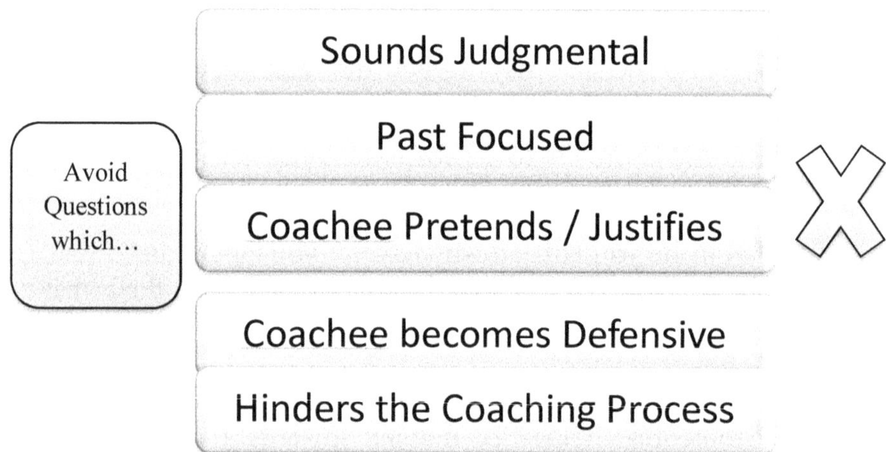

Golden rules for a great coaching conversation:

- **Paraphrasing:** To express the coachee's answer in simple, clear, often shorter and own words is called paraphrasing.

  This gives the coachee confidence and surety that coach is actively listening, acknowledging and participating in the conversation. Speaker understands that somebody is listening and responding with similar understanding. The trust factor multiplies. It can also be quite focused to the context as a summary of many lines uttered.

  Speaker: You know, I have handled many such similar situations in past and every time I have taken it head on and won.
  Coach (Paraphrased): Wow, If I understand it correctly, you have always been a winner in similar situations.

- **Metaphors are excitors:** Metaphors are an extension to paraphrasing, it's an art of reframing words which excites and influences client's growth and success. Most noted leaders and coaches, therapist use them in conversation. It's a great tool to match similar or identical persons, situations to draw quick picture of what may otherwise may not be clear. Coach picks up metaphors for exciting the conversation.

  'Your mentor's voice was like music to soul'
  'The world is a stage and we are the actors'
  'See like an eagle'
  'You might be falling from the sky into a gorge'
  'Don't think like a fish in pond'

- **Power of Pause and Silence:** To ensure best productivity of any conversation, pause after your questions and let the answer flow from the coachee. Answers always may not be prompt and immediate, coachee may require to think and go deep in thoughts. Silence prevails and it's the golden.

'Ah-ha' moment where the pause and silence ensure GREAT answers.

Pause and Silence is planned and deliberate art . In midst of engaging conversation, when ears are eager to hear and mouth ready to say, practice silence to ensure conversation is given depth, takes control of the situation, a simple answer can now be clearer, relaxes your body and mind. Mind processes more than 150 words/minute to speak and 4 times more to think. Pause ensures you don't use fillers and drag answers long.

- **Acknowledge and appreciate:** Acknowledgement of the answers can be the first point of building the conversation. Verbal and non-verbal gestures confirm the same. Hearing the speaker saying and accepting the views with simple gestures of a nod of head or saying, 'I see.', 'Ok' or 'Yes.'. The moment you acknowledge the interest on the conversation grows.

  Appreciation is the best tool for reinforcing confidence and encouragement. During a coaching session, remember coachee comes as a complete entity and has all the answers. Discussion would prompt several stories, memories and achievements. Do not always expect of big and large achievements for appreciation, a small and tiny aspect of coachee's happiness on efforts done should be appreciated and encouraged. It connects and rewards instantly the efforts. Highly recommended in coaching conversation.

  'That's sounds so nice…. really appreciate your efforts'
  'I am amazed with your spirits'
  '……for a moment I wonder, could I have done such good work ever'
  'Wonderful story'
  'Great inspiration'

Coachee to talk and drive the conversation:

"Coaching session is in service of the client / coachee"

Coaching conversation is always in service of the client or coachee. It is the session where coachee's progress is the essence, coachee's success is the desired outcome and the above viewpoint should be the guiding principle.

When session is in service of the coachee, LET COACHEE DRIVE the conversation . Let the coachee open up bit by bit slowly and think on the ways of solution. When coach starts to drive, there is hurriedness and confusion. Session gets bound by sudden time urgency and spoils the outcome.

As mentioned earlier, coaching session should encourage coachee speak around 70-75% of the time and coach around 25-30%.

- **Keep it Simple and Light:** Conversations are enjoyed, as the coachee talks, the joy emerges on the gradual discovery. Do not overstep and keep heavy discussions throughout, such process makes the session very formal and too formal atmosphere, debars coachee to speak out. Often an internal coach does not have great coaching conversation as invariably the formal attitude creeps in or business discussion overlaps.

  Keep is simple, share a lighter story, share a good movie or clip and ensures the atmosphere is made lighter. You can slowly increase the seriousness but do not make it very heavy as it may tend to make the coachee go overthinking post the session.

- **Seek Permission:** All humans are sensitive to many personal traits. It's a wrong assumption that during conversations, all questions are taken in the same spirit and understanding as coach may be in or coachee would have taken it in the same spirit as coach assumes. Hence seeking permission is a great tool and taking approval before asking something. It's also at the coachee's discretion to approve or say further. In case he/she has a discomfort in

saying more about something, please let that question go and its absolutely OK not to focus on things which isn't pleasant to coachee.
'May I ask you something about….'
'Can I seek permission to ask you…'
'Would you like to have a feedback on this ?'
'Is it Ok if I share my observation on this..'

Coaching Tool- 9. Journaling

1. What are my top goals for in next 3-5 years?

___

2. What are my top goals for next 10-15 years?

___

3. What is my goal this year?

___

4. What can I plan for next 3 months to achieve my goal this year?

___

5. What do I need to resolve now to ensure I carry the action plans?

___

6. How will I ensure I am on my way to achieve the plans?

___

7. What can I start this week which is top priority?

___

"What got you here, won't get you there"

–Marshall Goldsmith

COACHING GOAL , PLANNING AND ACHIEVEMENT

Chapter - 4

"Challenges become hurdles when GOALS aren't clear"

"Clarity of GOALS are foundation of success"

We have discussed so far, the need of coaching and the process of doing so, the focus is to arrive at a process to lead the conversation to growth and success. GOAL setting is one of the biggest milestones in the journey, BOTH the goals and the process of attaining it.

Conversation can begin with 'what is that we are set to achieve today?', 'what can be the goal we can achieve in the session?', 'can we define the goal we have?'. The process of finding and discovering the goal would be the most important during the coaching process and needs more pre-deliberation on the actual status, need and want.

Coaching GOALS give the following clarity:

- Focus on the importance of achievement in your personal and professional life

- Coaching blind spots in the goal discussion exclusively
- Goals re-alignment, re-adjustment, re-defining connects with your individual vision, purpose and values.
- Defining goals are like putting your dreams in paper and see them
- It gives enough details, visualizing and your control around it.
- Choices and options also become clear
- Confidence starts reflecting
- Tentative idea of time frame emerges in mind
- Attachment to goals grows which ensures your speed & eagerness

Let's have a quick assessment of our goals:

Coaching tool – 10.

Sl.no.		**Rate yourself on Y(Yes) / N (No)**	
a	I know I have many goals and I hope to achieve it	Y	N
b	I know my goals but appears as a dream	Y	N
c	I am yet to find out what exactly I want to do	Y	N
d	I start with finding what I cannot do, I get deterred	Y	N
e	I feel my goals are too small vs. others	Y	N
f	When planning, I ignore my personal life	Y	N

g	I fear a deadline, hence my goals are indefinite	Y	N
h	My goals are not detail oriented	Y	N
i	I change goals as soon as I see one hurdle	Y	N
j	I keep moving, but not satisfied when miss the goal	Y	N
	TOTAL	Total - Y Total - N	

The more Y, reflects to look back at goals and get coached for clarity.

Goals can be large and can be small. Coaching conversation focus on defining the goal and decide the present 'NOW' and the goal planning is nothing but the 'THEN'. ***The conversation is the path.***

Goals are the foundation of the journey, as a coachee one can have various thoughts about a goal and goals often have various connotations, as a coach it's important that

- Set goal early in the discussion
- Coaching journey has to have a goal
- You can define the goal as per best suited to coachee
- Change the goal also if the alternative goal is better
- Goal should follow the process of SMART
- Make goals simplified
- Break bigger goals to smaller goals and sub goals
- Make all intangible goals to tangible ones
- Goals need to be measured and have a time-line

- Sometimes, a conversation can just proceed with a goal-free discussion (this is only when a goal hinders the thoughts initially but eventually needs a shape in subsequent sessions)

Goals for every situation would vary, some goals can be simple and some can be arduous. Some can be for immediate requirement; some can be for short term while some can be for long term. Some goals may not be definitive and quantified.

Goals plans can be like:

- I would like to complete this job
- I want to start my own business
- Being healthy is my goal
- To be the best performer in my work
- Be a good leader
- I want to improve on communication
- Would like to complete the work by 6 months
- I want to start a new version of my life
- I would like to earn better
- Being independent in my thoughts
- I want to be extrovert in nature
- I want to be the head of organization in next 5 years
- Which job should be better for my career?
- How can I be popular with my work?

There can be therefore anything and everything which can be a goal and one which would be your real need. Goals can be categorized as

- **Short- or long-term goals** – I need to complete writing this poem/ I want to be the head of organization in next 5 years

- **Performance goals** – I want to be extrovert in nature
- **Vision goals** – I want to be a great human to be remembered / I would like to serve for animals / I want to plant 10K plants
- **Life Goals (Health/ Career/ Relationships/ Family/ Finance/ Spiritua)**
  I would like to see myself reduced 10 kgs by next year/ I do not want complications on health after 50 years/I want to outshine my appraisals this year/ I want to be a VP in my organization/ I want to find a have a great family life/ I would like to plan a car next year/I would like to be financially independent/ I would like to find peace and connect with my soul/ I want to drive happiness in what I do.

How you a Coach be a catalyst to your goal?

This needs a broader understanding and you can refer the need of coach and coaching on the previous pages. Coach ensures and deliberates the goal with coachee (do you really need this as a goal, how important is that for you, how would that be helpful, are you having all the essentials for the goal etc.) and goes through the coaching process, methods and continuously tracks along with you on the process of achieving. Without a coach, often the goals are not understood, planned, defined and tracked on the actions. It's a radar which navigates you till you have reached the destination.

GOAL setting process:

Out of the many processes of goal setting, SMART goal process is one of the most popular. While some be aware of the SMART process, would explain the details during the coaching conversation to be clearer and ensure it's the blueprint of discussion.

SMART

SPECIFIC MEASURABLE ACTIONABLE RELEVANT TIMELY

- ✓ **SPECIFIC:** Goals are positioned towards a focused outcome. Discussions can go all over in the beginning, it's the responsibility of both coach and the coachee to be focused on the goal which is to be addressed now and which is urgent. If a large goal is focused, small goals can be further dwelled on and set specific goals towards the larger goal.

  For example:
  'I want to be healthy' can be a large goal. 'I want to work towards being physically fit with .... BMI' can be a specific goal.

  'I will be able to do the work', can be looked at 'I will be able to work 16 hours per day on this project for next 15 days' can be more specific.

- ✓ **MEASURABLE:** Goals need a mechanism of quantifying. If goals cannot be quantified, it may sound vague. Any goal which can be looked into the progress tracking need to be quantified in some respect. Behavioral may be quantified in terms of happiness index, MBTI Index etc.

  With the above example:
  'I want to work towards being physically fit with 24 BMI (Body Mass Index)' is measurable with 24 being a parameter which can be checked in several instruments.
  A certain parameter, score, target, number, amount etc. can all be index to the count.

- ✓ **ACHIEVABLE:** Goal planning should start with existing and available resources in hand. With the available gifts of resources, constraints if any, goal should be focused on 'HOW' to be achieved. Focus should be on the outcome and all probable hurdles should be overlooked.

  With the above example:
  'I know I have limited equipment for exercise but I will see what I can do without them, as I have now taken a goal'

- ✓ **REALISTIC:** Goal planning has to be realistic. The process sets on post conversation as the coachee keeps on doing what has been planned. Goal planning need to more achievable.

  With the above example:
  'I want to daily wake up early and exercise to be more fit .... but you know I just cannot get early from bed'.

  A more realistic question can be asked, 'What is that one thing you would like to leave in order to achieve the goal'

  Realistic goals are more detailed with constraint understanding and what needs to overcome. May be in the above example, it can be just to overcome sleep. Here there is a check on whether the plan is doable or just a hypothetical plan.

- ✓ **TIME BOUND:** All goal planning needs a time frame of completion. Time frame depends on the type of goal, nature of challenges and agility of the coachee. Coaching discussion narrows your actions to more detailed time limit which can ensure faster achievements.

  With the above example:
  'I want to achieve a BMI of 24 by next 3 months'

  3 months is the time limit for the achievement; however, it is always recommended, coachee decides the time limit

and commits to it. If coachee want to revisit the time frame for increasing or decreasing, it should be accepted with more in-depth commitment of actions in the time frame.

Larger goal, can have intermediate shorter goals and intermediate shorter time bound periods. Ensuring all goal short or big has to be defined with a time and plan on the progress.

Remember:
"A small success with a shorter time line, is a success to celebrate in the process of large goal achievement".

With the above example:

'I want to achieve a BMI of 24 by next 3 months'
But, 'I will target to achieve a BMI of ……. by next 20 days in order to align to the bigger goal'

DISCOVERING GROW MODEL:

Whose GOAL, is it? Coaching conversation would be focused on again and again on the goal reference. As a coach, manager or boss, you would be looking at how best to assist the coachee towards the goal. The drive and enthusiasm is not the coach's, it has to be the coachee's. GOAL excitement, enthusiasm, hunger has to be the coachee's prerogative. Hence the clarity of ownership of goal and the drive has to necessarily be with coachee. Here coach's drive and enthusiasm is unimportant. Till the time this is clear, conversation can be halted for further progress and deliberated on .

6 Pillars of Coaching Conversation Methods – PEIRTR ®

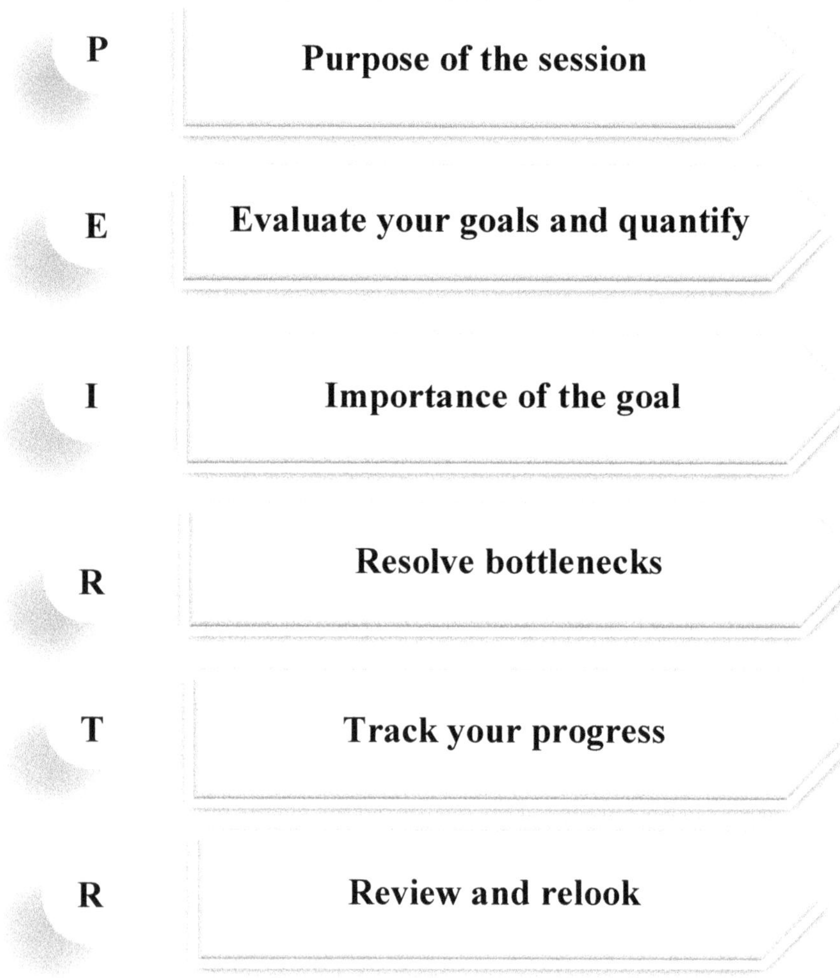

Coaching sessions are essentially a process of discovery and solution. Each discovery would be revelation and needs better understanding. Each conversation has to go through all the 6 steps of process above and form the core of discussion. These steps reinforce the flow with an outcome and shapes the conversation towards a fruitful result.

Purpose of the session

- Session starts with a clear understanding of the purpose and objective of the coaching discussion. Stating the core purpose is always the outcome which is focused. The flow of events would move around the focal point of the purpose or outcome. A purpose is the governing objective.

Evaluate your goals and quantify

- Goal as discussed earlier, has to have a mechanism of tracking. The purpose of the goal should have discussion around how it can be evaluated, measured or quantified. Discussion should spend time on how the goal can be measured, evaluated and looked into time and again.

Importance of the goal

- Coaching conversation aims at the purpose and narrows down to the goal and action. Discussion about a particular goal needs more detailing and understanding from coachee's perspective. Goal has to be important in one's his/her life. There has to be a bonding and obsession with the goal as its personal achievement. Goal has to be important and exciting to achieve, coachee should consciously or subconsciously own and drive it. If the importance is low, achievements are compromised.

Resolve bottlenecks

- Coaching with the goal in focus drives a detailed micro action plan and each action would be around certain resources. Resources vary across individuals and their personal challenges and bottlenecks. Any goal would have certain assumptions which may be overlooked or un-noticed and can become a hindrance for the smooth conducting of action plan. Arousing awareness of the probable bottlenecks and planning to resolve it before ensures better approach.

Track your progress

- Actions derived out of the conversation towards the goal would have various checks and parameters of whether it is proceeding as per plan. Since it has a timeline of conducting and completing, there needs to be an internal assessment of the progress which is planned. A quick tracker would help the progress and monitor it continuously.

Review , relook

- Goal achievement process would be seeking a continuous review and needs to be reviewed and relooked. Goal once set may look to be refined or re-defined after a day of doing it. Often time line drawn looks to be relooked after the first intermediate milestone. Such occurrences are common, however its always an effective method to review and relook and ensure progress is made unidirectional and goal success is achieved.

(Concept of TA101 can be looked to ensure each step front is sure, in case of any doubt, can be looked back at the last step and then relooked front again after review)

Let's work on all 6 pillars with an example for clarity:

Example: 'I want to be physically fit post covid recovery'

1.	2.	3.
Purpose – I need to see myself to be better, physically fit and having better immune internally.	**Evaluate/Quantify** – I would like to reduce 10 kg of weight and also reduce certain parameters of Blood Sugar Count / Pressure etc. (there can be some target)	**Importance** – It's so important to my life, I know how it affected me. I felt I should now be more focused on health, my diet, exercise, immunity.
4.	5.	6.
Resolve- I would like to prioritize my schedules and fix schedule daily for 30 mins for walking. Oh, I would leave my bed early now and find that extra time. Also, I would give up eating some junk food.	**Track-** Every day I am putting up my 'schedule' calendar I will monitor what I did daily on exercise, food etc. This will also inspire me daily. By end of 1 month, I will count by vitals.	**Review-** I have been good on exercise, I am still not going good on diet, I will now plan to stop ordering junk food as I see getting lured for it. I have also asked my spouse to see I am able to maintain it.

Conversation with the above flow would open many thoughts and actions. Coaching conversation can be done by anybody but the whole essence of the effective coaching is ensuring 100% awareness and 100% actions and review of the plans. Trained coaches are mentored on the same for years and understand the result well before the session and ensures it is always focused.

As a look towards an outcome and a possible action with a solution, as briefed earlier small positive and rightful solution can be looked as a milestone achieved.

Some quick awareness:

- Do you now see your goal? – a visual appeal
- Can you see the achievement?
- Do you feel the success? – kinesthetic appeal
- Can you hold the award?
- Do you hear the success applauds? – auditory
- Can you now hear what your family is saying?
- What steps you can now help you go faster?

Coachee becomes confident and tries his/her best with the internal awakening. Actions are now ***owned*** by coachee . Conversation can be stepped up with more finer and detailed asking:

- Appreciate your plans for next 2 months, can you help me know what are the actions you would like to do next 10 days?
- What are the first few steps you would like to do today?
- What can be your motivation towards starting your work today?
- Can you reflect on your thoughts to start this week?
- What percentage of your actions we can be sure by next 10 days?

Coaching Tool – 11.Let's try the PEIRTR Model

Your sample goal –

____

1. Purpose –	2. Evaluate/Quantify–	3. Importance –
4. Resolve	**5. Track-**	**6. Review-**

All above questions are **Call-to-Action**. These questions invariably would urge the coachee to look at making the action work. It will now change few things:

- Coachee's body language changes slowly
- Coachee's tone may also change with confidence (Refer tonality in previous pages)
- Coachee recalls his/her coaching even post session
- Coachee is focused on action and the tracking internally
- Coachee knows I can always reflect back to coach for any doubt
- Coachee decides on stronger will, with stronger words 'I will do it'
- Coachee's small success will now become his/her biggest achievement
- Coachee's trust on coach increases
- Coachee can come with more refined action plan with details as he/she would have dwelled more in the action, let him/her go that step
- Coachee looks forward to the next session for discussion

As a coach, the transformational change is a path which I say as the **'Re - Engineering Self'**

Coaching is a gradual process of change and the change has been rightly put forth by famous psychiatrist Elisabeth Kubler- Ross on grief cycle which can be a quite in sync to the change process in coaching process.

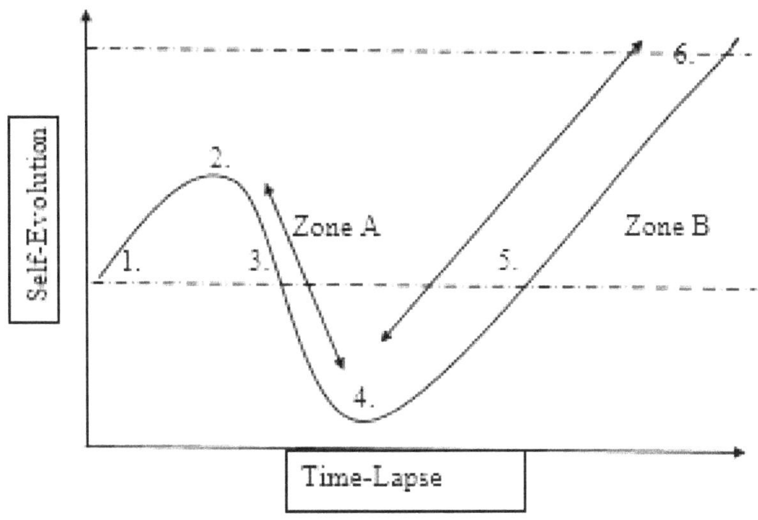

'Re - Engineering Self'

6 States of Change dynamics in coaching cycle

The above representation was highlighted in the Kubler Ross cycle which may be similar with respect to the change dynamics in coaching scenario.

There are 6 phases and should be understood. The trend of coaching conversation goes through the cycle of changes. The reverse 'S' can be different to each individual; however, the phases of changes are the real awareness and stimulate the change dynamics in behavior and habits of a person.

X axis represent the evolution of an individual

Y axis represent the time lapse of change

1. **State of Reality** – It is the state of present. It is often mistaken as a state of shock or grief but it is a state when a person accepts the situation and is facing the reality. The

reality can be a happy state also. It is the time when the coaching conversation starts.

2. **State of Denial or Non-Acceptance-** This phase is when the coaching conversation starts with raising awareness and many facts and data points are not accepted. Here a person can be a state of superficiality and may deny certain facts. It can also be a state where a person is overlooking certain reality and making assumptions arbitrarily.

3. **State of Uncertainty -** This phase is when your goals look clearer but path looks tough. Goal looks very tough, challenging, difficult. It's the time when coachee tend to give up and move ahead, plan different, switch plans and find easier ways. The goal looks uncertain and can fill anyone with anger, frustration and fear.

4. **State of Low** – It is at this phase when all realities, goal and action look clear, but since initial actions and sub-actions aren't showing early success, the is the state of mental low where a person is feeling the lowest on energy, motivation as the task or goal looks daunting and very difficult.

   Zone A (Phase between State 3 and 4)
   Phase is from an assumed high potential assumption of goal to finding it too difficult on the action plans and tendency to give up. Losing on own confidence.

5. **State of Ignite** – This phase marks the turnaround of the coaching journey with an ignite. Ignite of own energy, seeing small and incremental success of achievements and you start your process of taking ownership of the goal and action plans. This phase marks the upward turn of coachee's behavior and sparks of rejuvenated energy. This is the phase when you start taking charge of your decision, you experiment with various options, take responsibility and lead your decision.

(Most vital amongst all the states)

6. **State of Control and Growth** – This phase is when your confidence peaks and results visible. This phase can be your Goal No. 1 success or a sure path to upcoming success. Here onwards the path is well travelled and crossed various states to arrive at a point when you do not look back and chances of failures are negligible. It's a point when coachee starts on his/her path and coach slowly detaches. An excellent phase for both the coach and coachee where each know what is being done, yet both are not being guided. State of control is the ultimate stage of a coachee's success in the coaching process and the change is sustained. The coachee may look at different changes in the similar process and the trough can be less deep, however it will have all the 6 phases.

Zone B (Phase between State 4 and 6)
Phase is from an assumed low potential assumption of goal to finding it slowly possible and taking actions. This phase slowly unfolds the real U and ensures you achieve success and control and sustain it. I call this phase the complete – ***'Re -Engineering Self'***

Level 1 vs. Level 6 is a growth which is much higher and taller on where you started.

Time lapse – can be understood with weeks and months. Ideally the process can be 3-6 months or even longer or shorter depending on the coachee taking charge and actions. Failures can be mitigated if state of low is well understood and coachee do not give up.

NB*: All individual may not experience all stages and it can be direct path of 1-6.*

Coaching Tool – 12.

Sample Goal Planning Sheet:

My Goal No. 1	In order to achieve I would like to do these:	In order to achieve I would stop doing these:	In order to achieve I would start these:	What is the timeline I can plan to achieve?	I tracked the plan, it is as per plan (Y/N), if N, then a new timeline

Enneagram - Personality understanding for Coaching

Enneagram is a tool for analysing personality of an individual. It is a depiction based on what I am and what I need to improve on.

Every person has an inherent personality and need a basic understanding on

- What is my personality type?
- What is the other person personality type?
- What skills are required for communication, behavior for maximizing interaction for getting the best out of it

It was introduced as early as 1915 by George Gurdjieff, a philosopher and teacher meaning 9 (ennea) grammos (symbol) and later by Oscar Ichazo in 1960 who was able to depict in the modern avatar. It defines strength, weakness, fear, motivators, influencers.

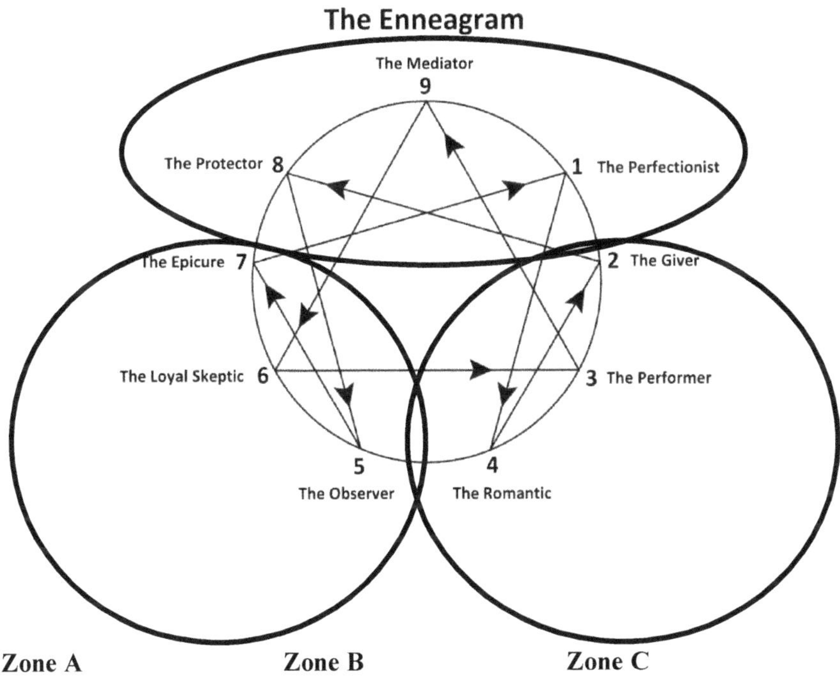

Zone A	**Zone B**	**Zone C**
2. The Giver	5. The Observer	8. The Protector
3. The Performer	6. The Loyal Skeptic	9. The Mediator
4. The Romantic	7. The Epicure	1. The Perfectionist

Zone A is referred as People with Heart

a. **The Giver** – They want to be liked by all, feel too bad when rejected
b. **The Performer, Achiever** – They want to be successful and want to be admired, want to be seen valuable
c. **The Romantic, Individualist** – They aspire to be unique and want to be different to others.

Zone B is referred as People with Head

a. **The Observer, Investigator** – They seek understanding and knowledge, seek data
b. **The Loyal Skeptic** – They want to be always secure, prepared for eventuality and fear non preparedness
c. **The Epicure, Enthusiast** – They want fun and joy and fear pain and sadness

Zone C is referred as People with Body

a. **The Protector, Challenger** – They are strong, powerful and fear being powerless.
b. **The Mediator, Peacemaker** – They want to follow, passive and fear pushing their own agenda
c. **The Perfectionist** – They follow rules and believe doing right things, fear being imperfect

Enneagram analysis can help arrive at the personality type and a combination of various other types of overlap personality. By identifying the true personality and the overlaps of other traits, coachee figures out the strength and the fears that he/she need to overcome. Building questions and awareness about reinforcing strength and ensuring you have plans for shaping out of fear. As a coach it is a process of gradually identify limiting beliefs and work on strength for sustained success.

DISC - Personality understanding for Coaching

DISC model of behaviour was introduced by William Moulton Marston, a psychologist in 1928 and later in 1940 by Walter Clark. DISC is a self-assessment tool.

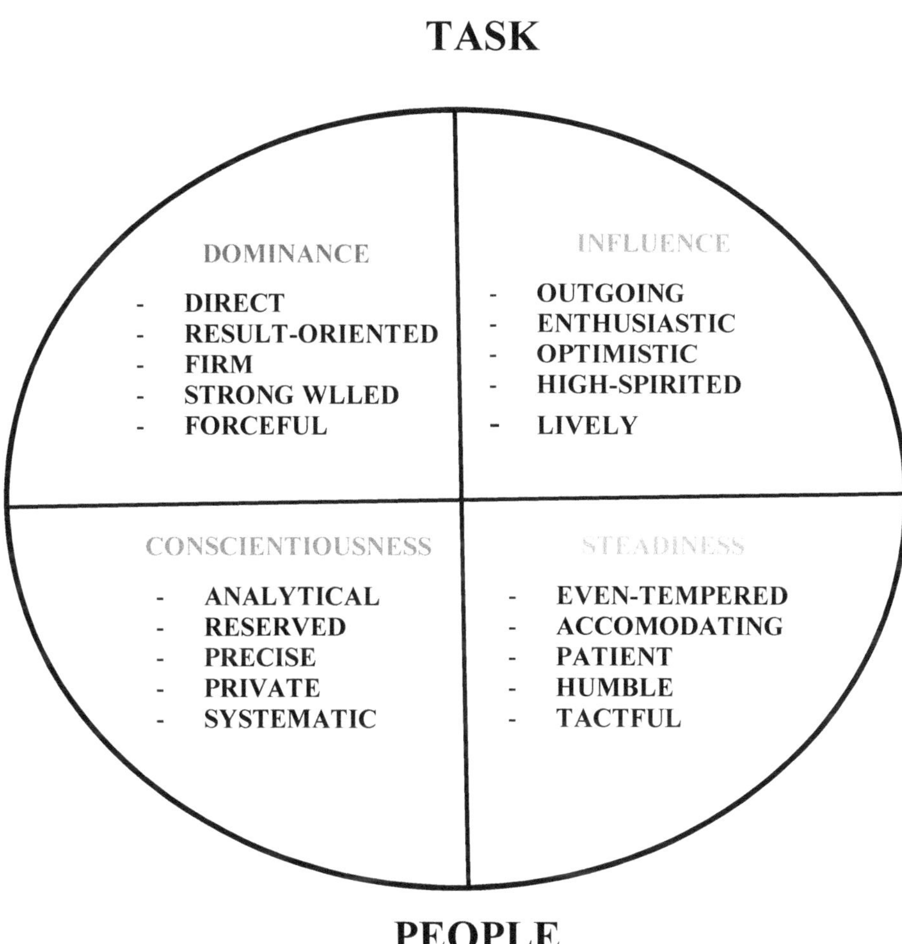

DISC assessment has major 4 personality which further can have further 12 personalities combinations which may have one major trait and one or two minor traits.

1. **Dominant** – These persons exhibit dominant personality and emphasize on result accomplishment and shows confidence. They see the result achievement and may ignore detail or people therein.

2. **Influence** – They believe in influencing or persuading others. Enthusiastic, likes collaborating and do not like being ignored.

3. **Steadiness** – They believe in cooperation, dependability. They are calm and are supportive. They do not to rush for result.

4. **Conscientiousness** – They are accurate, quality conscious and are detail focused, enjoy independence. They fear being pointed wrong.

Coaching focusses on coachee's personality and the need to plan and study people around and shaping up various question ask, communication and reaction plan for achieving a particular result and camaraderie.

"Champions never complain,

they are too busy getting better"

- John Wooden

Coaching Models and Processes

Chapter - 5

Behavioural Coaching Model:

Behavioural coaching addresses the executive leader on aspects which formerly form the inner core of humans. These are where it is identified the need for coaching which has larger objectives of goal alignment and contribution to the organisation. It addresses psychological and philosophical aspects of leadership grooming. Subjects which can form the core of behavioural training can be:

- Emotional intelligence
- Interpersonal skills
- Communication both verbal and non-verbal
- Ambiguity and conflict management
- Values and ethics
- Professional presence
- Accountability and responsibility
- Decision making – correctness and speed
- Team collaboration and building
- Drive motivation and energy
- Negotiation, presentation, articulation
- Change management
- Active listening
- Drive for results – mental preparedness
- Crisis management
- Adaptability
- Empathy
- Prioritisation
- And many more …

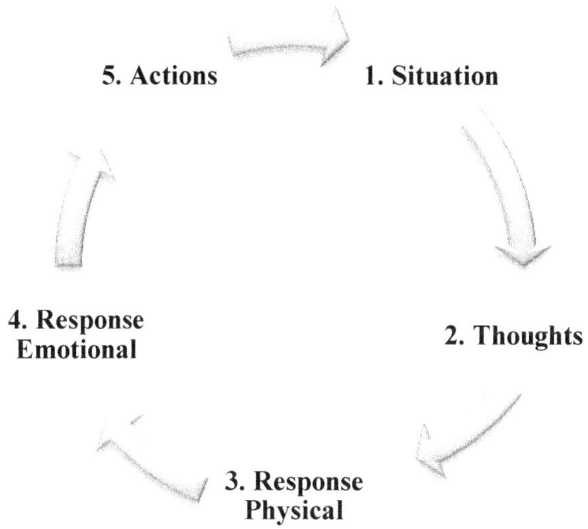

Cognitive behavioural cycle

The 5 stages can be explained as under

Example can be across

Situation - What is the trigger for the problem?

Thoughts – What is going on my mind?

Physical Response – What is my body reaction?

Emotional Response – What is my feeling towards this?

Actions – What is my action taken post this?

Popular Coaching Process

Coaching has been emerging and evolving with time. Psychologists, Trainers and Coaches, Doctors, Business leaders, thought leaders and others have time and again contributed to various tool and methods which define a process. These processes are often backed by a familiar acronym and each alphabet further signify or defines the sub process. The whole process is easier to understand and remains glued to the minds for longer duration of time and in turn.

1. This model was developed by me in my early years of coaching and it makes quite a distinction with respect to modern coaching styles. This model is a quick process of ***knowing, doing, repeating success.***

VISIONS

VISIONS® will always shape your coaching vision

V – Visualization of your goals.

As briefed earlier, all goals need to be visualized and seen. This technique gives clarity of knowing what you are thinking and planning. You can draw a goal, paint a picture, write your goals or just keep it in active memory. This should be your start to entire process. Writing, painting or just drawing gives some clarity to goals which may be otherwise hazy.

I – Instill the Will

All goals have to start with you, coach would take you only when you have the WILL to do so. The will is built on how strong and important is your goal and the eagerness to achieve it. Instilling the will can be the solid foundation thereafter to see the success of the goal.

S – See your options

This brings you to the point when you start to view the options at hand and gauge your best instinct and the various advantages and disadvantages for a particular option. Selecting the best option is the start of now acknowledging all facts and making yourself ready for the process.

I – Initiate the actions

This step calls to take the action after knowing your best option. This is where you start seeing the work towards your goal. This step has to happen with clarity of the action and the sub actions in it. Each of the steps would be with many challenges and hurdles but the action has to happen and continuity to be maintained.

O – Overview the progress

Progress needs to be checked by you on what actions was planned and what has been done. It may happen the pace is not in sync with the plans but it should not be the priority concern as long it is giving results. Overviewing is important or you lose traction of the actions.

N – Noting the natural flow

This stage should now help you for your natural flow to happen. It is at this place, that some new habits have started and some old ones are not maintained or left. New ones are good ones and are helping you on the flow. The flow should now be sub consciously done to ensure the actions are repeated without you doing with a force. This is the biggest change from your start.

S – Sustain success

This is when flow changes your habit and habit forms a change in your character. Every success only happens when there is a visible change and change which is good need to be sustained for continuous success. Every goal thereafter becomes easier and success becomes natural.

2. Developed in 1980's by Business Coach Graham Alexander, Alan Fine and Sir John Whitmore.

G	**R**	**O**	**W**
GOAL	REALITY	OPTIONS	WILL

One of the most popular and most used in personal and professional coaching. So, what does this model speaks about.

a) **GOAL** – It points directly to the targets or destination where you need to direct your energy, your focus. A milestone that is aimed at. This can be any destination that may be appearing before you or your passionate dream. This is critical to have a clarity of goal early as to be sure what am I chasing? looking forward and to reach. Goal sets in a clarity early in the conversation which leads to specific questions and discoveries. You can use the **SMART** goal setting described earlier.

- What can be a session goal today?
- What is your immediate goal in sight?
- What does this goal mean to you now?
- How important is this goal for you now?
- How did you arrive at this goal?
- When can you arrive at this goal?
- What will you achieve out of this goal?

- What was going on in your mind while visualizing it?

b) **REALITY** – It's a quick check on the status 'now'. The initial chapters of the book have highlighted a coachee's 'now' status as the start of coaching. Goals can be anything and can be big, large and bold. The reality cross-checks yourself on the status vs. the goal. Reality brings to the present moment and gives you an idea that would be your complete path from present to the goal.

- Where are you with respect to your goal?
- What is your current status?
- What have you worked till now towards your goal?
- On a scale of 1-10, how would like to rate your current status?
- What is working good now? What is not working good now?

c) **OPTIONS** – This step opens up various choices and selections on what can be the next plans. What plans may work, what may not. What actions will be productive or counterproductive. This stage opens up your thoughts and looks around for all possible corners for the best move ahead. It helps you to visualize which can be the best way to go ahead now.

- What are the ready options now towards the goal?
- Which choices do you see opening before yourself?
- What are the pros and cons of this option?
- Are you sure about this choice?
- Is there any other option which we haven't worked on?

d) **WILL** – This is a ***call-to-action stage***. You have worked so far on goal – you know your current reality – you have weighed all options and selected the best for you, now it's a call to take the action. You have debated, discussed your possible advantages and hurdles. This is the time when you go all out and make this action plan as a must do and carry out.

- When can you start the action now?
- What are the few steps you can do this week?
- How confident can you now do this action?
- What can you commit yourself on this action?
- What can be your first few steps now?

If it can be closely observed, each of the above process can be discussed with any goal you can have and take to the action steps. There is more detailed sub process to each but this method is a sure working strategy.

3. Developed in 1980's, **FUEL** coaching model was developed by John Zenger and Kathleen Stinnett, this model addresses behavioral and philosophical coaching needs, more addressed towards BEING coaching

- **F** – Framing the conversation
- **U** – Understand the current state
- **E** – Explore the desired state
- **L** – Lay out a success plan

4. Developed in 2000's, **OSKAR** coaching model was developed by Mark McKergow and Paul Z. Jackson is directed towards solutions.

- **O** – Outcome of the coaching that is expected
- **S** – Scaling of the situation on scale of 1-10
- **K** – Know-how and resources available
- **A** – Affirm plan and take action
- **R** – Review what worked

5. Developed in 2003 by Angus McLeod, **STEPPPA** model is process with context, emotion, action working towards a goal.

    - **S** – Subject
    - **T** – Target
    - **E** – Emotion
    - **P** – Perception
    - **P** – Plan
    - **P** – Pace
    - **A** – Adapt and act

6. Developed by Peter Hawkins in 1980's, **CLEAR** model.

    - **C** – Contract
    - **L** – Listen
    - **E** – Explore
    - **A** – Action
    - **R** – Review

7. Power of **JOURNALING**

    Journaling is a standard practiced tool in coaching. It's a process of depiction of what going within you as a thought, certain experience, feelings or you procrastinate. It can be widely used for any anxiety, stress or overthinking of a situation or anticipation of certain success or failure. It brings the coachee to the NOW moment when one is mindful of the status and draws some relevant conclusions of these thoughts and actions. Most of the journaling during a conversation can be written which coachee can reflect later as well. It's a practice which can be done for any situation, makes relevant conclusions, de-stress and gives a visual look to the plans.

- Morning Journals – the best time to be aware of and plan, write and review of goals and actions, track the progress
- Periodic Planners – Weekly/Monthly/Bi-Monthly/Half-Yearly/Annual - Chose which is better and relevant for your actions and goal plans, a reflection can be important to review and analyze.
- Questions and Prompts - powerful and most used in conversation
    - What is the way you would like to see 1 year hence?
    - What is the way you would like to see 5 years hence?
    - What is the way you would like to see in older age?
    - What are the actions you would like to do 1 year /6 months/ 3months/ 1 month / next week from now?
    - What would you do today for your goal?
    - What are the 3 teachings you would like to give your children?
    - What are your most proud moments in life?
    - One of your biggest achievements which no one knows
    - One of your biggest achievements which all should know
    - Imagine as a super hero, what would you do for the world?
    - Few things that your children should remember you for?
    - Pandemic has taught me ....
    - Biggest learning of my life has been..........
    - One thing which won't change anymore ....
    - One thing which can be changed now ....
    - I love my job as it ....

- I like to face challenges because …….
- I feel afraid because ……….
- I feel happy for ………….
- I feel energized for ………
- My dream for society would be ……….
- My dream for myself would be …….
- Relate to your best movie star, what do you like most?
- What are your top 3 things to do before you die?
- Assume yourself as parents, what would be their advice?
- Assume yourself as boss, how would he/she react?
- Assume yourself a mythical character, what would he/she do?
- Honesty to me is ……….
- Why is your family important?
- Whom do you run for advice and why?
- Tell me more on how to win the match?
- Tell me more how can be fit?

Most of the above questions and many more can take the perspective to a larger dimension and making it written makes you realize the actual status of it.

From FEED-BACK to FEED-FORWARD

Feedback is information which is a reaction to a particular product, person, a task or a reaction to a situation which generally talks about an improvement. Feedback has been common and as humans we are most of the time ready for feedback. This is an important process in a coaching journey as it reflects back to what is perceived, understood or status post an action.

There can be feedback based on

- Feedback on results
- Task based feedback

- Performance based feedback
- Encouragement based feedback
- Conditional feedback
- Nonverbal feedback

We will understand **Feedforward** better here as an important change. It is almost reverse to feedback. It was coined in 1980's by Peter W. Dowrick . The concept was developed with cognitive and behavioral science. Negative or positive feedbacks are replaced by forward and future paced solutions, ideal fit to the coaching process. Marshal Goldsmith on his various sessions and books have highlighted the change process to feedforward from the feedback orientation.

FEEDBACK	**FEEDFORWARD**
• *Past focused*	• *Future focused*
• *Elaborates the past occurrence with details*	• *Suggestion and improvement discussions prevail*
• *Critical analysis of the event which is over*	• *Analysis of development and progress is focused*
• *The feedback provider speaks most of the time*	• *The feedback receivers speak most of the time*
• *Errors and mistakes more emphasized*	• *Focus on 'what', 'how' can be done better and improved*
• *Takes a judgmental purview*	• *Coaches on task not person*
• *Coachee feels bad at times and may not open up*	• *Coachee feels comfortable and opens up, participates*
• *Environment is very serious*	• *Environment is very encouraging*

Let me elaborate here:

As a manager, one figures out that he should provide feedback to his team member as a process, 'I see you need to improve on communication' as an example. This may be simple feedback but is not at all clear as to what exactly and how to do it. In the feedforward process, now the manager is asked to say only things ***what he can do in future to improve*** communication.

Now he may say 'Look you can start writing emails shorter and crisp' or 'You can improve your pronunciation in conversation' or 'can you improve speaking slower and clear' and many more. Now in the second process, no comment on what has happened or what was the past occurrence. Rather as a manager focus was to assist the colleague on what are his observation and how can he improve so that his communication can be better in general. The effective work now by this team leader would be more clear, more practiced consciously towards improvement rather than doing many hits and trials across.

The feedforward is an encouraging session of engagement of looking ahead, forward and what can be done better instead of spending too much of attention on what's already happened and what does not necessarily give enough ideas for what next to be done. As elaborated on the representation above, people would be more attuned to hearing:

- What can be done to improve certain areas in future (how)
- Shifting mindset away from 'what went wrong' to 'what can be right now'
- Initiating a positive change with self-acceptance
- It does not become a personal remark and push back the coachee to think
- Change is visible post this
- It can be applied across all areas and practiced during common sessions

It's a change in communication pattern with qualitative approach, must adoptive for leaders in all streams.

"Real Leaders are ordinary people with extraordinary determinations"

- John Mattone

Coaching Scenarios and Consciousness

Chapter - 6

LET GO OFF

Let go off is an important milestone covered during any coaching conversation and has a huge significance.

What does 'let go off mean'?

Let go is to leave or dissociate yourself from certain thoughts, beliefs, situation, expectation, person or an experience. It is to leave that back and move forward. Most of the mentioned thoughts, beliefs, situation, expectation, person or an experience can be holding you back on certain plans, decisions, emotional attachment, bonding, new steps or any new experience or person.

Let go off can be also to not to pay any attention consciously to a particular thing, person or trigger. It can also mean to forget and march ahead. It may also to just let things take natural course of flow and limit, leave your control on unwarranted aspects.

Let me explain you:

- I heard you want to stay healthy and have morning exercises, what would you let go off to plan your schedules?

Here it means, what can you forget or go away with. It can be laziness or morning sleep or late night keeping awake which hinders your waking up in morning and go for the walk.

- You want to be a full-time entrepreneur, what would you let go off to plan your goals?

Here it may be to leave your full-time job or leave your 'only planning stage' and start doing something or it can mean to go away from your comfort zone.

Goal planning has to have this component of 'let go off' plans, which needs to be seen in details which hinders your progress. Coaching conversation, focusses on the goal and tries always to remove all hindrances and things which are presumed to be hindrances.

Some more examples:

- I would let go off my sleep, in order to achieve good marks in exam
- I would go away with my smoking habit to be healthy
- In order to be organized, I would let go my habit of being cluttered
- I want people to know me, I will let go off my introvert nature
- I would let go off my fear in order to achieve this goal
- I would like to forget my past failures in order to plan better now
- I would let go off my pain, in order to be a great boxer
- I will now let go off my feeling of being the center of influence
- I will let go off my pride, I see successful people so humble
- I have to do this now; I have to let go off that feeling of failure

In order to achieve something, coaching reflects introspection on what all can be 'let go off' moments to have bigger achievements. What can be your 'let go off' details on these criteria.

Coaching Tool – 13. LET GO OFF

HEALTH	
I want to hold on with	**I will let go off**

INFLUENCE	
I want to hold on with	**I will let go off**

CAREER PLANS	
I want to hold on with	**I will let go off**

GOALS	
I want to hold on with	**I will let go off**

PLANNING PRIORITY	
I want to hold on with	**I will let go off**

RELATIONSHIP	
I want to hold on with	**I will let go off**

How to coach self from fear of failures:

All of us would have seen failures and success in life. While we cheer during success and feel bad during failures, it's the circle of life and would continue every time with every person irrespective of place and background.

Let me reflect back again on the Indian mythological Hindu scripture of "The Bhagawad Gita" of Chapter 2 verse 37, written 5000 years ago.

Hato vā prāpsyasi swargaṁ jitvā vā bhokṣhyase mahīm
tasmād uttiṣhṭha kaunteya yuddhāya kṛita-niśhchayaḥ

It translates to:

If you fight, you will either be slain on the battlefield and go to the celestial abodes, or you will gain victory and enjoy the kingdom on earth. Therefore, arise with determination, O son of Kunti, and be prepared to fight.

The verse speaks about the understanding of challenges and how we perceive it, it is as simple to know that if you accept the challenges and know how to face them and fight, you will be able to see the wonders of success.

- Had it not been the arduous pressure of the seeing the light of Independence, Father of Indian Nation, Gandhiji would not have driven all his energy towards making India independent in 1947. The Goal of seeing a new India was all it had.
- Had it not for 10000 failures, Sir Thomas Edison would haven't invented the light bulb. Only he knew what are the ways it will not work and one way it will work.
- Had it not been the goal of Karoly (Olympian from Hungary in Pistol Shooting) lost him arm in 1938 and went on to win Gold in Olympics 1948, 1952 with one arm.

Coaching to overcome fear can be looked with few essentials:

I) Learn to know why somebody would have failed in certain endeavor. What would have been the shortcoming if any? What would have been the learning out of the process?
All leaders do mistake, every person does so. It is these mistakes which ensures you learn and try not to commit the same.

II) Analyze and understand the root cause of the failures. The result of the outcome may be negative, but many small steps would be done correctly. So, what went right and what went wrong can be a good analysis for ensuring coaching focus is on the analysis.

III) Set the expectation and goals clear to resource available and competency which can be addressed. Re-focus on goal early in the conversation and adjust your actions.

Empathy and Sympathy in Coaching

"Empathy is all about seeing, hearing and feeling for others"– Self

You must have come across these words of empathy, sympathy, compassion in your leadership and life skills understanding. The need to discover these more is important as coaching has deep insights with these value systems.

Sympathy is a feeling of compassion which is felt when somebody has pity over a person or situation. You start feeling bad of something which you feel is not accepted by you or is difficult. It's a feeling of personally going through something when its heard or seen and share similar feelings.

Empathy on the other hand lays is a wider experience of other's emotions and sentiments which you feel without feeling pity but more so with a similar stand point of feeling.

For example:

Sympathy : I am sorry at your business loss; can I be of any help in this moment?

Empathy : I heard of your business loss, I had been through similar moments last year too.

Sympathy :As a doctor, I was pained at failing to save the patient

Empathy :As a doctor, I know this therapy would be painful but you can speak to so many who have been cured and are happy

How can it relate to coaching?

During a coaching conversation, it may be very natural to hear something which you feel bad, worse or utter pain. At such situations as a coach, you may feel to jump to something which can help to heal the pain and start mentoring and giving advices. Such advices aren't needed as coachee may not accept some feedbacks which may be emotionally incorrect and may dent the relationship. This is when you start feeling sympathetic.

In a conversation, where similar case has triggered some bad experience, it's important for the coach to hold on to the nerves and not allow to flow with the pain. It's important at this juncture, coachee needs solace and need to be carefully be taken into 'what caused the pain', 'what was the action', 'what can be done to prevent' and 'what has been the learning' so as to be always prepared for handling such a situation with firm and bold attitude.

Empathy is the skill which you slowly acquire as an individual be it in your personal or professional space. Clarity of coachee's feeling, aspirations and concerns are understood with similar stand points. It's a quick acknowledgement of the status of the coachee but at the same time leading to more logical discussions to either come out of it or emphasize on the learning to avoid similar situations. Being over empathetic or sympathetic alleviate the coachee's condition, it can go further and further and enter in zone where return constructively would be difficult. As a coach you should guide but also you cannot be too attached or sink in the moment being over empathetic.

Remember: It's a coach job to take the coachee to the zone of success.

Advantages of being empathetic?

- Improve relationship
- Build one-to-one rapport
- Co-create atmosphere of safety and collaboration
- Build respect and trust
- Speaker, coachee can speak and release tensions
- Conversation is deeper and hence actions would be meaningful
- Growth and forward-looking thoughts emerge

How can anyone practice in conversations to be more empathetic?

- Active listening
- Active presence during conversation
- Listen beyond the words
- Do not jump to give solutions
- Acknowledge with simple words and gestures
- Hold your nerves being sympathetic and ask some simple questions, 'I empathize', 'What was that......?', 'What was your feeling then...', 'It must be scary.', 'I too have goosebumps' etc.
- Analyze the situation
- Participate in the conversation
- Ask some questions like 'I heard you......, what was your best learning?', 'It must be really bad, what did you do after that', 'what is the best teaching for yourself', 'what can you do to not let it happen again?'

Last few questions arouse awareness thereafter for looking ahead, rather than dig more in past. Coachee tries to assemble the thoughts now to look ahead for progress.

Coaching for Stress Management

"Stress is a simulation of thoughts – pick wisely"

Stress is a common to all and appears in every session across any personal or professional development plan. Huge time is spent on elaboration of stress, symptoms and the related effects which at times are obstacles to growth. In this book we would discuss about coaching for better management for stress.

Evaluate coachee for their professional, personal domain, emotional, relationship, health, well-being or people management areas and gauge the levels of stress one has, or is going through or anticipates in future.

Coaching Tool – 14 . Are you under stress now?

Try and rate these for yourself:

Sl.no.		**Rate yourself on 1(Low) – 5(High)**				
a	I am an easy go person	1	2	3	4	5
b	I believe in the 'now' moment	1	2	3	4	5
c	I do not worry much about my future	1	2	3	4	5

d	I fall asleep fast and sleep for 7-8 hours	1	2	3	4	5
e	I eat good food and exercise regularly	1	2	3	4	5
f	I love humor and enjoy lighter moments	1	2	3	4	5
g	I am very happy with my friends and family	1	2	3	4	5
h	When I get hurt , I usually don't keep it long in my heart	1	2	3	4	5
i	I do not react immediately and roughly on provocation	1	2	3	4	5
j	I spend good time with a hobby or leisure time	1	2	3	4	5
	TOTAL					

Scores which are higher above 30 tends towards higher stress and should be looked into.

For Example

'I do not worry much about my future',

Everybody would be worried about their future and needless to say everybody would be having some thoughts around it. There may be very few who do not worry at all, some may be worrying about it sometime, somebody would be worrying often and continuously. A score of 5 is a great art of knowing it, but not worrying about it. A score of 1 can be a concern where the primary focus is future plans and it keeps bothering both consciously and subconsciously. What can be the coaching plans and asks here, assuming score of 1 of a coachee.

Some asks can be: - (not in sequence)

'What do you exactly worry about your future?'

'What does your future plans look like?'

'Tell me more on it?'

'What has been your strategy so far to handle till now?'

'What is your expectation which you would like to do?'

'What can make you happy that you are on track?'

'What is the time period, you have planned with it?'

'What if, it does not match with your plans?'

'What are your options?'

'What are your key challenges?'

'What have you done so far to mitigate the challenges?'

'What are those expectations once you achieve?'

'What alternatives you can think for ensuring you do better?'

'What can you let go off if you need to achieve?'

'When can you pat yourself, that I am on track?'

‘What can you do to ease out your bigger plans into smaller ones?’

‘How important is that for you?’

‘What if you stop worrying …. will that not happen?’

‘What if you …. plan less?’

‘What else can help you reach…?’

Few of the above asks and many more such thoughts can assist the coachee on looking at things in a broader perspective, details which is needed and details which may not be needed, what if it does not happen, what if I plan less, what can be the assistance which I can seek, what can be some smaller goals planned and what can be some actions which can help me from continuous worry. Similarly other deliberations can be acted upon and most of the stress related points can be eased out gradually.

Please refer again to ‘The Bhagwat Gita’ sloka mentioned in the beginning of the book, where the reaction of self to the situation is ONLY under your control. The event is not under your control, the outcome is. Your reaction is in your control, if you let the reaction be dominating you, stress can overpower you.

More realizations:

- What can I do to be focused on what I do good or great?
- Am I aware of my own talents?
- What makes me happy, have I done that.
- All decisions are fine, there is no wrong or right
- Is the worry for me is also for others?
- If it’s not for me, then can I control?
- What if I start with the worst result in mind?
- Do I have all means for that, if yes let me work on it, if no what are the way I can acquire them or seek them?
- I am aware stress is the trigger of various diseases
- Is my stress hampering my own growth?

- Is my stress hampering my relationships?
- Are my near ones happy when they see me?
- Am I the only one in such situation?

The coaching tools which are explained in previous pages will navigate you with the planning and easing it out.

Coaching for your strengths

'Your strength is to start with ...Yes I can'

Coaching based on strengths has gained momentum across world primarily for the focus it gives to an individual on the his/her potentials and competencies. Strength based coaching focuses on the 'what' and 'how' of the core areas of an individual. It is based on positive psychology and the laws of affirmation.

How does a normal assessment look like?

ASSESSMENT OR APPRAISAL OR COMPETENCY MAPPING	
Areas of Strengths	***Areas of Improvement***
• 1 • 2 • 3 • 4 • 5	• 1 • 2 • 3

It has the areas of strengths and areas of improvement. None has the area of improvement blank or vacant as per all the assessment studies, various mapping of professional or personal mapping of competencies. That means everybody has strengths and improvement areas irrespective of position or personality. In coaching context, coachee strength areas arise from the values, purpose, beliefs and the behavior which is in the inner core explained earlier. Strengths are those advantages which an individual has. Why do we need to focus more on strength? Because it engages the positive sphere of energy, garners positive psychology, fosters feelings of joy and success and connects with the inherent potential of the individual.

- Strengths are natural outcomes and hence should be maximized
- Areas of improvement are important, but more focus on strengths can outweigh the improvement areas
- Strengths uses higher frequency of growth in brains
- Strengths can be modulated for growth, use and transfer
- Strength's coaching will emphasize on clarity, passion, optimism, confidence, result orientation

During coaching conversation, therefore the focus should be to groom on strength and assist coachee to dig deeper into how strengths can be improved and utilized.

What strengths I may have and can be proud of? You can relate to yourself, each sentence fosters positivity and grooms forward looking attitude.

- I am honest and loyal
- For me, being healthy means all
- I know how to plan my funds and be financially happy
- For my career, I am on track on my plans
- I have added skills and knowledge to be always competitive
- I have great relationship as I nurture them well
- I remain optimistic and inspire others
- To find happiness in everything I do, motivates me
- I trust people
- I take efforts to be compassionate
- I go beyond my means to help others

- I always try to find solutions when I am faced with a problem
- I believe in sharing and giving
- I love to take challenges in life
- To run away is not in my character
- I appreciate punctuality
- Discipline is honorable
- To forgive is divine
- I care for their feelings
- I am proud of my achievements
- I feel happy to share my learnings to inspire others
- I know to how to present what is being asked
- There are happy moments which I would always remember
- I would remember the success stories and repeat
- I am ready to take up new assignments
- I learn from basics and stick to fundamentals
- I can communicate well
- People confide in me
- I know how to motivate others
- I know how to live life full
- Public speaking comes naturally to me
- Analytical strengths are my greatest gift
- Proactive thoughts keep me moving
- Inspire and transform is my motto
- The show must go on for me
- Every day has a new beginning for me
- I know how to plan and take risks

Coaching for growth mindset

'Anyone who has never made a mistake has never tried anything new' – Albert Einstein

Growth is the essence of the coaching outcome and all coaching gives a clarity on growth as it evolves. Growth of the outcome can be mapped separately to each individual. As my thoughts in this are concerned, growth necessarily in coaching means expansion of his thoughts, his beliefs, finding the awareness of current status, planning goals and consciously moving towards an outcome. The efforts and knowledge which coachee drives during and post the process is, planning growth and the will to drive pushing your inner and outer core is the mindset.

How does growth mindset improves coaching*:* It's a beautiful question, took some time to understand and delegate to others. In our current dynamic environment of emotions and counter emotions, continuous performance and deliverable demands it's not easy to just know of the areas of improvements. It's a plan which is to be put to unlearn, learn and relearn skills and techniques, groom self on competencies, plan personal growth story and readily adopt coaching strategies would not be easy. If success and the need for success is understood, the action plan becomes auto driven, growth mindset emerges which is hungry to put forth changes and remakes for self to emerge as winners.

'Growth mindset drives the momentum as a catalyzer'.

Coaching Tool – 15. GROWTH MINDSET

Are you having a growth mindset? Try this questionnaire.

Sl.	Situation	Personal Assessment		
		True	**False**	**Not Sure**
1.	I try for new things for change and innovation			
2.	I know I can't do it and hence do not start			
3.	Smart people are born talented			
4.	Smart work does not need hard work			
5.	I make mistakes, I learnt from them			
6.	I quit when going gets tough			
7.	I act more than I plan			
8.	I plan more than I act on			
9.	I feel hesitant for new experiments			
10.	I update my skills and knowledge			

The answer for each of the above would vary to each individual. Positive outcome and growth driven mindset encourage action and innovation, people would like to plan and implement, are ready for new methods, do not generally quit with failures, they track their own progress, set and changes boundaries to the need of the situation, encourages self and others for challenges, deliberates on options, has risk appetite and seeks new ideas skills and knowledge.

How can you coach for growth mindsets?

One of the biggest contributions of a coach is to assist the awareness of coachee to think holistically, think bigger, think beyond the hurdles and boundaries and think of how to face the challenges better, take proactive actions. To cultivate:

- Encourage growth thoughts and talks
- Small mistakes are Ok, learn and avoid
- Plan, Do, Check and Act Cycles (PDCA)
- Workshops for innovation
- Out of box, out of domain learnings
- Begin with end in mind, mitigate risk plans
- Active listening and understanding
- Update skills and knowledge
- Seek help, knowledge and acumen
- Practice mindfulness and meditation

Coaching for Conflict Management with Individuals and Leaders

"Conflict is the beginning of consciousness"– M. Esther Harding

Across the world, data reflection on personal and executive coaching points at one of the top reasons what needs coaching is conflict management coaching. Is it good or bad or healthy? As the quote above reflects, conflict is the beginning of consciousness and consciousness is the seed of awareness which is the first step towards coaching effectiveness. Conflict in today's world is nothing new, we all would have in our personal and professional life. No conflict is in a passive zone where growth stops. Conflicts is one of the ingredients of active and proactive growth.

Healthy conflicts and Unhealthy conflicts are to be understood in a broader perspective of how the conflict unfolds and shapes up. If it's a constructive process which arises out of non-agreement of certain points and ideas and results in evolving the entire process which in turn adds to the qualitative growth is a healthy conflict. One which does a destructive and long standing detrimental effect is unhealthy and needs to be avoided. Conflict management therefore has been a part of competency management tool and appears in most corporate and personal coaching.

What's the benefit of conflict coaching for an individual?

- Focus on self rather than him or her
- Behavior and its responses across people
- What could be the source of conflict
- What can be handled, how can be handled
- How people vary in communication
- Engage and collaborate
- Better understanding
- Resolution planning for win-win situation
- Know what to engage and what to disengage
- Proactive thinking
- Building self confidence

Discoveries with coaching here:

What actually needs coaching?

- It's not about winning all conflicts; maturity is to be open to perspectives
- It's not only your emotions or judgements, it's a step towards collaborative and proactive thinking
- Avoiding is not the solution, participation with your active thoughts is leadership
- Not to be critical analyst but an adaptive change leader
- Respect every individual and their thoughts and look for a collective win

Coaching for Resilience:

"Bouncing back is a natural ability, use it more when you need most"

Resilience is preparedness as a spring and building agility to bounce back in adversities. Setbacks, passive moods, feeling low, shaken confidence, feeling of losing and many such negative feelings would be common to all individuals. These moments are natural as bouncing back is also natural. The lower you feel as a coachee , remember you would be bouncing back to your highest peak of success and turnaround . Resilience coaching is discovering the hidden potential of individual to bounce back, it's like lubricating your inner self and making the spring work better to bounce back naturally every time you face any low feel.

How Coaching helps here: Coaching as discussed is a discovery process of coachee's natural strengths, natural ability to handle, natural ability to find effective solutions and walk on the process.

Finding your natural strengths and strengthen it : This would be the most important understanding of what are my strengths and how do I know it . What are the ways coachee can strengthen it with the best available resources? Natural strengths can be

- Your control on your emotions
- You lead any initiative
- Your ability to develop relations
- Your ability to nurture relations
- Your ability to think 'big picture'
- Your focus is on road or goal
- Your ability to motivate self
- Your solution thinking mindset

You can rate yourself on a scale of 1-10, to be at 10 are your strength and if its low, each can be worked on for progress

- **'CAN DO' Attitude:** Believing on your strengths encouraging self with a positive attitude can be a significant move towards being resilient. To start with a mindset of 'Can Do' gives optimism and develops any situation towards a favorable outlook.

- **Strong emotional balance:** Being aware of NOW and building awareness of WHAT can be completely wrong if emotional balance is lost. How can a balance be attained? Being worse or completely unaware of certain situation can push of the delicate sync which is so important of one's growth and emotional control. A strong balance would push a resilient outlook.

Coaching Leaders for Ideal Character :

Leaders are human beings and would be exposed to all spokes of the wheel of life defined earlier in different degrees. However, leaders are assumed to demonstrate high level of character in personal and public life which inspires many lives. Leaders are expected to lead with special strong character which not only inspires many but also makes the leader matured to handle future goals and challenges.

Coaching leaders for character would be a 360* development of a person holistically. So how does it happen? Character of a leader as any human being would be arising from inner core of value systems and positive beliefs and a very high level of integrity and commitment. Character build starts from early childhood and shapes quite early in many individuals whereas many would consciously build the same over a period of time. Character build cannot be cosmetic or artificially projected. Character is also checked by series of psychometrics assessment for new senior recruitments, new assignments or groom for taking leadership roles. What are the key elements being coached for a ideal character built?

- **Wisdom** – Wisdom is natural but can be coached to groom the same with intervention of 'thinking creatively', 'sense of judgement making process', 'knack for learning continuously', 'building perspective'.
- **Courage** – I would like to give good weightage to building courage as an ideal character. 'Strong decision making', 'Encouraging risk taking abilities', 'strong will', 'perseverance' would be ideal.
- **Loyalty** – is clearly the strong commitment to the cause. A goal is seen by the zest and vigor of the drive. People around look forward on how one is committed to drive despite all ups and downs.

- **Humility-** Biggest leaders have learnt this early. Being humble, modest is a great technique for being collaborative, respected and followed. Leaders pave way for open ideas, participation of all, manage all emotions, mix with all and keep the camaraderie alive for constructive work. Also coaching is essential for balanced temperament for great acceptance.
- **Gratitude** – It's a step after being humble whereas every effort of all including yours is well taken positively. Even mistakes give opportunity to learn and hence an open appreciation, knowing each effort is worth several manhours, struggle and practicing to appreciate and showing gratitude brings the leader with loyalists and committed team.
- **Motivation** – Not everyone knows how to motivate and energize. It's a skill learnt very hard and needs a through coaching process. Outcome dramatically changes with degree of motivation. Must as a character for leaders.

"Leaders spend 5% of their time on the problem and 95% of their time on the solution, get over it & crush it!" – **Tony Robbins**

Chapter -7

Executive and Leadership Coaching

What is Executive Coaching:

Executive Coaching is a one-on-one development of an Organizational Leader. It is one-on-one collaborative relation between coach and coachee , he/she is an executive in an organization interested in improving himself/herself in career , business or related skills. It may be defined also as capability building for yourself and your organization towards improvement of business outcomes. It can be looked at development of leadership acumen.

Executive Coaching may be directly be planned for Executives by

Organization-HR-Business-Executive driven - Coach

Or

Executive directly driven – Coach

When is Leadership and Executive coaching is sought:

- Leadership Development is one of the most important reason of most coaching needs across world.
- Leader in Transition – is definitive leadership development plan by the organization. May be a promotion in mind, change in roles, larger roles, international movement, handling mergers and acquisitions, etc.
- Retention and grooming of high performers – It's a win-win for employee and organization to continuously keep grooming talent for and make them ready for next roles in mind. Employee also see as a learning development
- Performance Issues – Usually employee is earmarked with poor performance and employee seem to be underrated without actually addressing the core bottlenecks. A remedial to development coaching and ensuring a 'come back' is one of the best employed tools by organization.
- Career coaching – Many a times, employee directly undertaking career coaching for self-development. A coaching intervention reflects a mirror to the coachee of his/her current status, preparedness and plans for his bigger goals and achievement.
- Delegation of Mission, Vision – Employees many a times seem to work in silos, a coaching intervention brings in place larger groups or departments within organization's common vision and mission or orient towards new vision or goals in case of re-orientation.
- Core – competency management and plans – organizations sometimes earmark executives who may be good to excellent in many competencies but would lack certain attributes detrimental to organization. Coaching contracts are very specific to these objectives and needs quite detailed discussion.
- Target / Goal Planning – organization often contract for target and goal setting exercise and plans for achievement with more detailed readiness.

How does this benefit the organization? 3-sided advantage

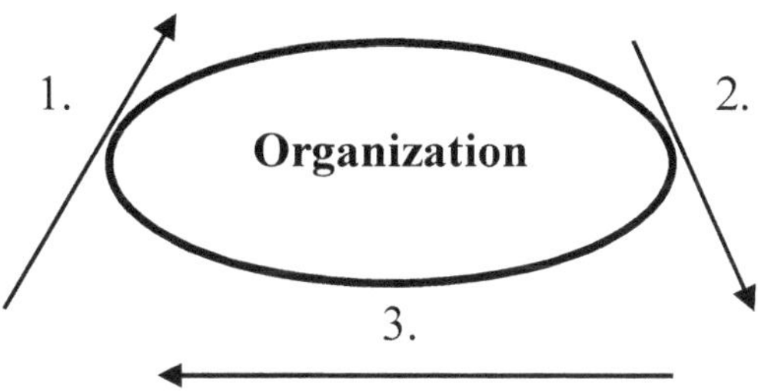

1. *Management* ***above you gets your development with detailed understanding on organisation's need****, vision, bigger picture and playing active role*
2. *Subordinates who report into you with a* ***difference in handling, communication, making the big picture clearer and actively participating into a team with clear goals***
3. ***Peers and similar levels*** *within departments* ***or cross functions tend to get better ideas and handling*** *of the same situation differently.*

What professionals go through internally:

- **Blame Game,** quite commonly understood across corporates and professionals and it has been an endemic. Leaders view it very often and often leave the subject without a concrete action. Blame is past focussed and will jeopardise professional's and organisational vision and growth. Lack of feedbacks and reference often derail it. Coaching focus is always for future and garner an optimistic environment for collective growth.

- **Stress,** seems one of the major challenges faced by almost all professionals. We have an entire section how coaching effectively address stress; the origin of stress is anxiety. Stress being the reaction of body to various physical, emotional and psychological strains in the work life. It may arise due to poor work-life balances, timelines, multi-tasking, poor management, improper work atmosphere, absence of healthy lifestyle, strained relationship, procrastinations. Coaching address each of the above with deep rooted changes which lasts forever. Executive look forward for awareness and management.

- **Lack of Support and Encouragement,** has been one of the growing facts which makes professional look at coaching. Coaching not only supports the status of the individual on his/her level of awareness, 'what' and 'how' to better equip self to effectively manage and also bring in a long-term vision plan for his/her goal.

- **Current management style of company,** debars both new and existing professional to look beyond the box. Professionals would be looking at learning and development, growth and knowledge upgradation but may feel at absence in their current workplace for either the organisation doesn't not support the objective or the current boss/manager.

- **Performance related,** professionals have been highly seeking the performance related coaching which would have aroused in appraisal cycles and would have been not attended. Performance coaching has been one of the most sought-after coaching programs in corporates or done at an individual level across professionals.

- **Being uncomfortable with change,** new norms, new organisation, new boss, new roles, new place, new work schedules, new department are a part of the fear that one has. The older one is to the comfortable zone the longer it takes for being uncomfortable and then settle down. Coaching addresses these symptoms and prepares professional for handling and engaging swiftly.

Individual Benefits of Executive Coaching

Coaching Federations has time and again issued several guidelines of benefits across various coaching assignments and executive performance thereafter, clearly its encouraging. The percentages are indication of improvement success for coaching interventions.

I) Improved self-confidence – 80-85%
II) Improvement of Performance at Work – 70%+
III) Improved Business Management – 65% +
IV) Improved Time Management – 60%+
V) Improved Team Effectiveness – 55%+
VI) Improved Work-Life Balance – 65-70%
VII) Improved communication skills – 75%+
VIII) Improved Relationships – 70%+
IX) Organisations which saw investment coming back – 86%
X) Individuals who saw investment coming back – 68-75%

Overall Satisfaction Rate of Coaching

99% with 96% repeat process of engagements

Coaching Need for Indian Corporate:

(Published on LinkedIn)

India has emerged greatly post-Independence era, with a socialist approach prior to 1990, scenario changed by start in 1990 era. Economic liberalization and globalization have changed the India corporate diaspora. The lag prior was subdued with the dominance of so called 'western management style' which was fast, effective and competitive. 1990 onwards the markets opened with globalization which was highly driven by customer centricity and service orientation, which also allowed higher privatization. The era post that to 2010 was a growth of Indian corporate going global. Infosys, Tata Group and many more showed the trend with corporates across world having many Indian CEO and leaders in their board rooms.

With a fast-changing atmosphere - what changes? In our early childhood, an average person dreaming for a car had clearly 2 options, Fiat or Ambassador. How are you gauging the space now? Flooded with more than 30 manufacturers with multiple variants and customers are spoilt for choice. So, it started a competitive environment, increasing customer needs to propose value for investment, short business cycles, constant need for technically upgrading and planning innovation in goods and services. So, across corporates the challenge to evolve daily, plan better, plan advance than others, deliver business in constantly changing complex environments. Senior leaders spending hours to plan sometime what's tomorrow now?

Evolution of Executive and Leadership Coaching: Coaching gained inroads over training with its effectiveness it delivered to Leaders. Corporate leaders across world found it as an amalgamated approached which has the integration of best of B-School knowledge, training and mentoring methodology, knowledge of several books - journals- courses which was coupled with one-to-one behavioural analysis, psychometric tools of assessments etc which touched the heart and mind simultaneously.

Although coaching is still nascent in India, emerging trend of Coaches in India clearly shows that no more a leader is 'shy' to tell that 'I have a Coach' which otherwise was felt quite contrary to what coaching delivers.

When going through Mr. John Mattone's program, I had asked him, why then Apple boss Mr. Steve Jobs would at all need Coaching. He clearly said that this is where he is in a space to push himself beyond the boundaries, fix his inhibitions and innovatively dream years in advance and all this with a clear understanding of your own habits, behaviour, strengths and what can be better done from what currently is.

Why the need for Coaching in Indian Corporate a must?

India is land of mix culture, a huge workforce which is educated and young. Campus intakes are primarily still based on purely academic and basic assessment-interview. Not many have the opportunity for an affluent B School or a mentor in life. Even senior management - CEOs and C-suite executives are lonely at top. With a humongous pressure at work, not many of the leaders discuss problems openly for fear of being perceived weak. Somewhere the Indian culture has a taboo that limits an open discussion in office. Sometimes it's taken wrongly as well. Coaching comes here with providing a safe atmosphere, which is unbiased, confidential, where coach becomes 'a friend for life' and gives a safe space for open discussion clearly sorting out one's limitation and fear, work towards strengthening core competencies. The skills and competencies that have brought the executive and the company to a certain level will not be sufficient as the company grows or as the executive moves up the career ladder. An executive coach helps the leader develop new perspectives and skills to meet additional demands that come with a change in responsibilities. With a growing millennium force - high ambitions and fast changing urge for growth, coaching is the solution to track and pace your plans vs. targets set both personally and professionally. Indian corporate scenario would further change from now to 2035 with high-speed broad band communication, hub for technology manufacture with China no more a favoured destination, medical and scientific innovation hub, services headquarters for many organizations with seemingly increasing start-ups, India is surely changing. So why the human force doesn't need a deep introspection on grooming to face the next decade challenges? India is in the command to deliver not only results in advanced technology but how to deal the humans behind all this. The need for Coaching at all levels at any corporate would overall change the performance output and see sustained results with the workforce.

The ROI of executive coaching:

Executive Coaching Process: KAAA – 4 Phases

1. **K – Know** your clients/coachee/employee – make them understand the coaching process and establish the objectives . Good time to build rapport, it's a chemistry of two minds which need a beautiful camaraderie, set some arousal of thoughts which makes the session to look forward to with huge interests. There should be discussions on expected outcomes.

2. **A – Assessments** of the Individual – there can be multiple channels and mechanisms of pre- assessments which we will elaborate later, however what should be assessed is more depth of the individual both psychological and potential mapping. These can vary across organisations and individuals like i) Anagrams ii) DISC iii) Hogan iv) Lominger iv) MLEI v) 360* vi) Thomas psychometric etc vii) Appraisal reports. While it's all about knowing the coachee in details BUT NOT forming any biased idea. Ideally any tool would be having a logic behind the algorithms and coaching assignment should not be formed on pre-fixed any logics. These only form a basic understanding for both coachee and coach to

work upon common gaps or strengths which is agreed upon.

3. A - Action – It's an important part of the journey when coachee reflects on all the discussion and awareness created. Coachee can start implementing the new ideas, behaviour, practice his refreshed communication, try new skills, reinforces his/her relations with stakeholders. Coachee starts grooming the changes and practice in daily routine. Periodic reflection and review on developments can be looked at, what's can be better. Spending many development workshops needed to groom certain skills and increase the awareness and learning curve. Coachee would ideally be discussing how the new ways are helping him/her or what can be added, what isn't working at all.

4. A – Achievement – a coaching process can have intermediate stories of accomplishments. These are somehow the boosters of the journey. Applaud, appreciate, acknowledge the feats and admire the new found changes. While the coach would be focussed on larger achievement, these stages can be the actual changes of the habits. Some session starts yielding results by 3 months, some by end of 7 months. Ideally there are no clear rules but the achievements would be continuing even after the sessions are over. Here the coaching contract would end with the major outcomes achieved in the stipulated time. There can be follow up, feedback and final report on the journey.

How Executive Coaching shapes leadership styles:

Lot of leaders, corporate executives and individuals who gets on the call have a rich background of academics, experience, various training and learning sessions and yet they asked 'should we really engage'. Statistics released recently by ***'Development Dimension International Inc'*** 2021 and ***ICF***

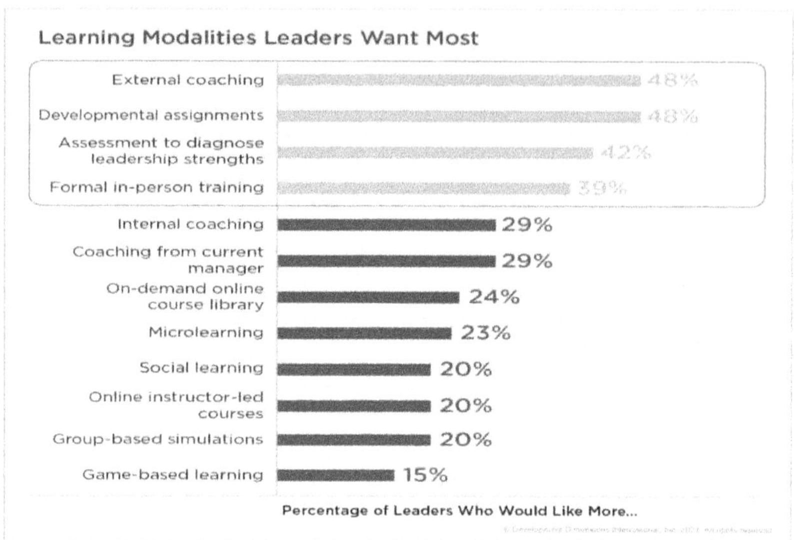

The focus clearly emerges on external coaches, executives and leaders have been clearly showing and affinity and its understood that it results in success.

Over the years, its shaped to the few inferences which results differently:

- Leaders clearly understand the difference between the potential, performance, current skills and need addressed
- They shape up acting strongly during crisis – coaching shapes them up slowly over a period of time on their maturity of understanding and reacting.
- They slowly become sharp on weeding out non-productive issues, time wasters and focus on result-oriented strategy.
- They slowly start understanding that that to get best results, be with the game.
- They arrange and re-arrange, re-calibrate members based on potentials and performance and shapes skills with deliverables.
- Potential can be elusive, its implication: predictive trait assessments that measure a leaders' enduring values and goals, behavioural tendencies and critical thinking—are all

very important measures that help accurately estimate a leader's potential. What also helps is seeing how they act and respond to the tougher situations and challenges that come with larger roles without actually being placed in the larger role (e.g., simulation assessments—assessment centres, on-line leadership simulation assessments, and behavioural interviewing are powerful tests of leadership potential—especially when combined with trait and critical thinking assessments.

- High potential can be looked at giving their best , look at succession and developmental decisions .

Do we need a Coaching culture at the workplace:

"Coaching is unlocking a person's potential to maximize their own performance. It is helping them to learn, rather than teaching them." – Timothy Gallwey.

A coaching culture experimented over the year across all organisations have resulted positively and being effective across. The interaction levels across senior and junior management where coach and coachee can be internal. Often a coach can be from a different department, function etc. There are quick understanding of action plans, review and feedback mechanisms.

- Coaching grooms' leadership qualities and showcase a simulation of what can be a future leader like.
- There is a synergy of work across organisation which becomes more energized, involved, takes ownership and puts the additional effort.
- A collective win-win mentality prevails.

- Employees become creative and also readily contribute beyond their domains.
- A high level of motivation across org prevails.

How to imbibe a coaching culture:

I have been hearing at several places, questions asked by leaders that whether we need to develop a coaching culture, why should we move towards that model of working, what would be the difference then and how effective it would be for the organisation in long run.

I find it quite messy that managers moving around and coaching people here and there, changing hats and starting to coach somebody and doing coaching. I am sure coaching culture is not what is assumed and it is not surprisingly that complicated and need so much of preparation and planning.

Anybody working with a manufacturing domain would have walked across shop floors and would have asked the mechanic as to what he is doing, how he can do better, how to reduce failures and how his output matters to the assembly line. Similarly, an IT manager would have walked past his team members and would have asked delivery, programmer etc and would have checked on progress, change of plans, testing the plan and making it effective to the client. What did these managers just do, **they coached**? Nobody knew what is coaching and nobody was exactly aware what they are doing is exactly coaching. Therefore, coaching is not new and should not be planned for a new change. It was always there; it only needs a new understanding and training behind it. Coaching, advising, mentoring, instructing etc would have all worked with these, now it needs to be trained that 'what now needs more to do' and 'what can be avoided'

Coaching culture is a transition to the 21st century management and the better, sharper and clearer we are on this, we know how to handle the work force and get the best output. What can be looked at:

- ✓ Leaders should be become the role model after their initial coaching assignment and learn the techniques and cascading plan
- ✓ Coaches build coaches – I strongly feel that that organisation cannot afford for entire team separate coaching assignments and hence, leaders, department heads or vertical heads can become the coach for the next level. Also, to keep in mind in the world outside coaching is agnostic to designation and hierarchy but within an organisation it can be done by a role leader above.
- ✓ Coaches who would be the starting should be ideally not from same function, department and should be able to demonstrate coaching before starting, otherwise may end up doing mentoring or consulting.
- ✓ Coaching should become the directly deliverable on people management skills of the manager. It should have schedule, efficacy, routine feedback and developmental work as review parameters.
- ✓ Often people management and coaching within organisation is taken low priority of business results, here the process itself would be not effective and would not result in the core objective, hence organisation should be very careful.
- ✓ Although L&D and HR would be the custodians, but it's the business heads who actually see the results, hence coaching routine and development be also as a part of the business head's deliverables.

Coaching Tool 16.

Self – Check on Executive Leadership Coaching Needs

Sl.no.		Rate yourself on 1(Low) 10(High)
1	How good have you been to achieve your goals vs your plans, targets	
2	How convenient are you to show caring nature at work?	
3	How good are you at building strategy?	
4	How good I have been to communicate in teams?	
5	My thoughts and actions are assertive.	
6	How good are you in motivating team?	
7	How good are you in presenting your thoughts and actions to seniors?	
8	How good are you in managing time lines for a work?	
9	How good are you in helping others learn new things?	
10	How much do your team members meet and talk with you for their personal issues?	

	TOTAL	

Indicative scores: Max marks 100

Please be as true as possible in your assessments, you may keep the results personal. To be more practical on the approach, assessments are spread over various parameters and may be much more questions than given above, however this may be just a quick reckoner;

- 90-100: You are doing good, keep it going high
- 60-90: You have strong potentials and need coaching for maximising your results
- 30-60: Need coaching interventions for competency and potential grooming
- Less than 30: Need longer intervention of coaching, training and competency planning

You must have noticed now that; I have spoken of competency and mapping of various skills.

What is competency? Dictionary meaning is the 'ability to do something successfully and efficiently'. More refined in workplaces, 'capability to apply your knowledge, skills, talents for the best delivery of work-related functions in the workplace. Competencies can be your internal core abilities which forms your habits and which governs your deliverables at various life circumstances.

There can be various references to the competencies which defines an individual with respect to any organisation. Dr. Marshal Goldsmith, one of world's most renowned thinker, mentor and coach and one of my inspirations always defines these characteristics. Later I have seen several organisations, coaches defining the core essence and shaping to various tools or 360*,

IDPs etc. To give a summary, any individual would be primarily carrying activities around 2 major aspect, PEOPLE and TASK.

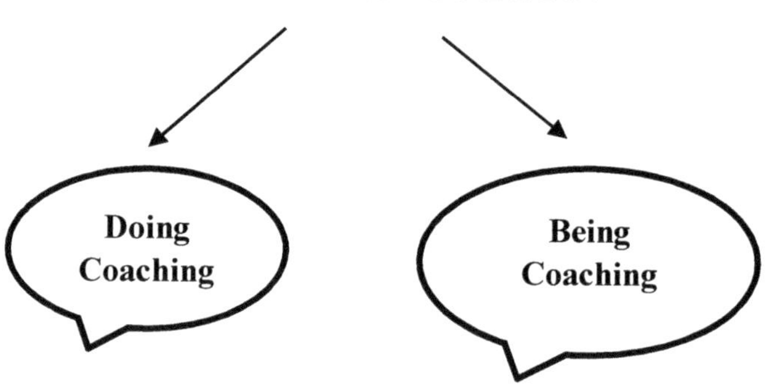

Common Competencies in Leaderships Can be referred as C1-C24			
1.	PC	Self-Management Skills	Effective communication approach / Interpersonal skills
			Exhibit high standards of ethics and integrity
			Assertive and share vision
			Value driven thoughts
2.	PC	Engage People and Team	Build teams and effective teams
			Engage creatively for effectiveness
			Imbibe leadership vision
			Develop teams at each level
3	PC	Social and Emotional Intelligence	Social Skills and response to variety of societal demands
			Emotional changes across people, compassion and empathy
			Courage, confidence -risk

			appetite
			Encourage equality, diversity
4	TO	Solution Oriented	Success orientation
			Driving modern technical advantages
			Infusing competitive edge
			Stake holder management
5	TO	Growth and Evolution	Resource management and optimisation
			Speed of decision
			Analytical on data
			Change management
6	TO	Sustainability	Best practices and process governance, go global
			Expertise teaching and refining
			Coach and Mentor

The Coaching competency mapping can be mapped through various strengths, assessments and simulations.

Competency Sl.no.	Rating Scale (1-10)									
C1	1	2	3	4	5	6	7	8	9	10
C2	1	2	3	4	5	6	7	8	9	10
Overall C	1	2	3	4	5	6	7	8	9	10

C - competencies which can be from 1-24 based on above

Based on various assessments, a coachee can analyse his strength or his area of improvements.

Is coaching the replacement for appraisal?

No, that is incorrect. Appraisals and coaching cater different objectives altogether. Appraisals are formal planned sessions for reviewing fixed KRAs or defined objectives versus actual efforts and results. Coaching is an highly interactive and integrated dialogue process, which is built to address the needs of KRA to achieve the result. It's a bridge between planning the result and defining the efforts with periodic checks and balances. I would say, coaching here synonyms with **Performance Coaching** which is to be done both at the start of the financial year, quarterly and periodically to review the progress .

Traditional Appraisal Process	Performance Coaching Process
Very Formal	Effective when Informal
Feedback, comments on topics with opinion. Often starts with what went wrong	Feedforward, start with what can be bettered or improved
One way dialogue, appraiser leads discussion	Coachee leads, highly two-way interactive session
Often result expected, rewards are spoken, 'how' part is missed	Focus on goal planning and with huge focus on process, removal of bottlenecks and optimisation of resources
Ends with Manager-Subordinate relation build	Creates a huge bond with coach focus on improvement of the inner core for sustained changes

Coaching for Change Management in Corporate:

Coaching for change management or coaching for development of growth. Many would be hearing it at various intervals as to what are the difference and how change can be coached.

Let me ask you a question. What do you think would be one of the biggest reasons why leaders fail when they have challenges? It has been one of thought which I would have analysed over various companies and their CEOs. One of the reasons which come across to me to the top of the list is the 'ability for managing change'.

Change adaptability has been very dynamic to industry and has reduced the response time considerably over the years. What corporates and leaders would have read or heard 10-20 years back, current speed of change would be faster? Anticipating huge influx of modern technology back with AI and software, it would have a further speed and would knock people off their comfort zone or assumption zone unless the mind works faster than anticipated. Therefore, understanding change and coaching change should one of the top priority areas of corporate leaders.

Coaching for change can be towards a new abnormal which becomes the new normal. Why do I say this? Change coaching starts at the end of the comfort zone and does plan audacious and abnormal goals. Few may seem that as stupidity or over ambitious, however to stay relevant for long, out of box thinking happens when you are in the uncomfortable zone.

You may have heard that a new CEO has multiplied the targets 5 or 10 times, a new leader directs having a new product or technology which they never had, a leader directs to multiply the customer base by 10 times or higher. As a coach these are the outcomes of a strategic thought which has a foundation for change planning. Change can be directed towards a new vision, target audience, new content, new culture, new mergers, accelerate process or a complete U turn for sustenance and relevance. Such coaching can be challenging as it drives change and change is always uncomfortable. Here's a quick way to adopt

Change goes through 3 process zone and the previous illustration of '***Re-Engineering Self***' can be looked at also.

Change Level	***Thinking status***	***Acceptability status***
Level 1	Easy	Difficult, Bad
Level 2	Difficult	Good
Level 3	Broad	Easier with new normal

Let me illustrate, 'I want to exercise'

Change Level	***Thinking status***	***Acceptability status***
Level 1	**Easy** – yes exercise is important for my life and I would like to do it.	**Difficult, Bad** – I have to get up early, reduce my sleep, remove junk foods
Level 2	**Difficult** – Oh my! Do I have to walk or run daily 1 hour to be fit, it needs lot of my efforts	**Good** – I have to do it , I am fed up with my weight and I have to do something about it.
Level 3	**Broad** – Now since I have started doing it, I feel I can do some treadmill, walk and run combination which also helps me similarly	**Easier with new normal** – I am enjoying my reduced weight and would never like to go back again to the previous status

Managers and coaches, need to coach on this understanding that these phases are must in change planning and levels have to be crossed to get the new normal.

Executive Coaching Process

The process is similar to previously defined process, however its more apt taking corporate guideline process:

Coaching contracts are looked at by Corporate HR / Business Leaders in different stages. The progress happens with multiple partners and sessions to finally see the conversation and session happening.

- HR and Business, identify person and the competency needs which needs grooming and sharpening, it can be in sync with business needs, expansion, long term plans
- Pre discussion with HR , Business , Peer and most important with the coachee on the coaching need identified
- Defining coaching needs and closing an agreement
- Analysis of all assessments, appraisal documents, feedback and if need be, design assessment-based plans for competency mapping
- Coaching session conversation
- Opening up of coaching conversation with need, importance and change management which coachee is aspiring for
- Arriving at goal, planning the detailed action plan
- Action plan analysis
- Progress report, review, needful amendment and feedback
- Review of scheduled actions and implementation
- 6 month – 1 year review mechanism, if need based can be more on time lines.

Executive coaching – Why it is effective?

Executive Coaching, Leadership Coaching is proved across world as an effective process and it is evident with the data shared by ICF and other bodies the coaching arrangement at various organisations and C-Suite leaders attached with a coach. As per various data shared by coaches more than 70% describe results from coaching as "excellent," and more than 70% percent benefitted from work performance & communication skills, leaders view productivity increase by 50% and profitability by over 25%. 96% of corporates opted for repeat coaching assignment again for overall gains.

Executive coaching and Impressive ROI (Return on Investment)

6 / 10 companies offer Executive and Leadership Coaching to Leaders. Impressive arrangement for coach involvement at a glance. Many organisations have asked many coaches across their journey on their ROI and its very pertinent to glance on the topic for clarity.

Coaching prepares leaders and takes on the journey of change and self-engineering as briefed earlier. Coaching assignment can vary from $100- to 4 figure or more per hour depending on the coach profile, his/her experience and the organisation and leadership profile. It is like a senior doctor and his associated fees. Studies across coaching organisations across world, coaches and organisation reveal 6-8 times of each $ (dollar) spent. It means the effectivity cannot be directly measured using few parameters of results. While there are coaching reports for analysis, focus on what the coachee started doing and adding to the organisational strength post coaching on long-term. Coachee's new found insights, his control on his vision alignment, performance orientation, communication improvement, team management and collaboration, productivity analysis, social management skills etc which cannot be measured in terms of money analysis.

In addition, coachee's understands various connects of work-life management, priority of both personal and professional urgencies, releasing stress, looking for a guide or guru in life, adding confidence and direction in life are much added benefits.

Executive Coaching is a smart investment for company's growth philosophy for both short term and long-term plans.

- Other studies indicate positive ROIs as well from Training Organisation and ICF also indicate a positive note of (55%-89%) improvement
    - Improved executive productivity
    - Improvements in organizational strengths
    - Gains in customer service
    - Increased retention of executives
    - Enhanced direct report/supervisor relationships
    - Improved teamwork
    - Improved peer-to-peer working relationships
    - Great job satisfaction

Of course, the ROI of Executive Coaching depends on the expressed desired outcomes for each engagement, the Coachee's willingness to receive information s/he may not want to hear, and the Coachee's own desire to put in the hard work to consider thinking (and then leading) differently.

As an Executive Coach, I've had the opportunity to see Coaching as a powerful way to expedite a leader's ability to impact business results. It is impactful because of the awareness it creates on the part of the Coachee, the alignment in thinking it opens for the Coachee, and its bias for action (results orientation).

Whether your desire for Coaching is solely for your own edification or whether it's also wrapped around a desire for increased sales, new accounts, decreased absenteeism, improved productivity, reduced workplace drama, better work/life balance, improved employee engagement, or something else, you'll find that Executive Coaching is a viable pathway to expedite your leadership and bottom-line business results. Coaches have been coaching clients with leadership development coaching sessions for more than decades and clients see the impact on their bottom line.

Coaching Senior Leadership

My discussion with Mr. John Mattone on this subject and coaching very senior leaders across organisations, I came with few discoveries which Mr. John mentions in JMIL and becomes quite relatable.

What are the coaching needs which a senior leader would look forward to other than the above? A senior leader would be visible across industries, fraternities etc, still what coaching needs still he needs to address

Mr. John while coaching Mr. Steve Jobs, the Apple CEO had various questions put across. A simple question to Mr. Jobs as to why a Apple CEO would need coaching when he would have achieved so much to be already recognised a global top company with best brand and turnover. At a level what could be the driver and what would be the vision, when you already at a No. 1 position. ***Mr. Steve Jobs replied to Mr. John "I was put on Earth to make a dent in the Universe"***. It took days for me to understand the CEO success and his continuous urge of the statement. The statement in whole defines a larger objective of an individual. This becomes the **CORE PURPOSE** of the CEO which drives his inner and outer core.

So, what's the CORE PUPOSE:

Core Purpose is not Vision and Mission of the organisation and its core values. Its more than just that. I would have thought deep being long with the Tata Group, as to why in India and World over, Tata Group commands respect, it's one of the largest conglomerate and people associate trust, confidence and remain attached for long, and its across their 100+ group companies. There's a strong organisational core purpose. Defining the core purpose of the organisation would be very intricate, most strategic for a leader. Some questions may be:

a) What is the purpose of our organisation?
b) What are we doing?
c) Why are we doing?
d) For whom are we doing?
e) What is the impact it creates for our stakeholders, customers, shareholders, business partners etc ?
f) Is the business model on push or pull mechanism?
g) What is the legacy left behind?
h) Is this unique of ours?
i) Is this legacy futuristic?

Once you start seeing the evolving of these answers, purpose become more defined. Therefore, PURPOSE is defined in simpler language as, 'it's an emotional, logical, statistical drive which you are doing for the larger cause of employees, stakeholders and society in large, leaving a legacy to the world'.

So how does top leadership associate with core purpose: It's the above questions which keeps driving a thought amongst all leaderships and striving for the best answer. Many CEOs would be defining and refining it during the course of the tenure to make to specific and attainable. Coaching becomes the best solution and constant source of soul search during attaining pinnacle of business success.

Queries which Leaders ponder on:

1) **Am I justifying my assignment here** – this is typical question which opens during conversation and leaders are so focussed on their contribution and partnership for the growth? Many leaders assume they aren't contributing or anticipate changes to come forth when this question would be more glaring. Hence the competency mapping needs focus and grooming. All leaders contribute, yet some leaders are constantly questioning their individual role. Coaching assignment addresses their position and prepares them for any future references of justification.

2) **What are my inhibitions and limiting beliefs which I need to forego**? Individual maturity also pushes certain inhibitions and beliefs aside and coachee may not be aware subconsciously. These limiting beliefs are born right from birth and gets influenced through grooming, schooling, teachings, experiences, societal stimuli and form deep within. For example, 'I can't trust this person, I don't know much about him/her', 'rich people don't know hardship' etc. These thoughts are groomed over a time and your behaviour is exhibited from it. Many targets and goals are missed because of these mind sets and hence needs to coached to first understand and then plan for giving it up, if it's not contributing.

3) **Have I addressed my blind spots:** This is a classic query raised by many leaders? While all leaders would have enough contribution and would applaud their journey, yet the boss would be helpful on certain areas of improvement or your assessment say so. To address them may be an intention, leaders drag the addressal mechanism longer. To be on a constant vigil about your blind spots and seek a coach's help to address them in due time ensures you walk the talk.

4) **What is my 360* feedback and how do I address the improvement areas:** many organisations have been sharp on 360* plan of action at all levels and the gradual cascade at all levels. A detailed 360* discussion follows for better understanding.

5) **I feel alone at times at my work place**: Would empathize with all here, organisations would have driven business for continuous results. Leaders across organisation would be driving on timelines, lack of guide and mentor at work, poor work-life balance, answering stakeholders suitably etc. I am sure many of the leaders would face them and seek lonely and stressed. This can be hugely addressed with coaching philosophy and continuous engagements to ensure this is overcome.

6) **Conflict Management:** Most senior leaders have shown across surveys that conflict management resolution and what can be the best process of doing it becomes high on agenda. Many a times conflict is avoided but the organisation decision is delayed. Addressing conflicts can get addressed the cause and root to most of the issues and drive the best outcomes. A quick view of the various issues.

Data reflected by major research papers for corporate coaching needs and why do they seek coaches. Most of the above data reflects on senior management requirements which may differ as we progress down the ladder. These would be some the most important coaching needs across the globe for corporate leaders across all bands.

- Manage Conflicts
- Overwhelmed with priorities and confused
- Race to over achieve and be top performer
- Focus on turnaround strategy
- Planning skills

- Listening skills
- Sharing leadership / delegation skills
- Team building and effectiveness
- Decision process
- Empathetic leadership abilities
- Motivation

We have discussed the second most important skill for coaching 'listening skills' which seemingly is across the board.

Leaders often feel that if business has to be driven, delegating it often may NOT give the desired outputs. As a result, business may be seen in control of few, results are also expected to be with few. As it's said, **'leadership is all about creating leadership',** power of delegation, sharing space with leaders, creating second in command who is equally empowered takes away huge chunk of the 'non-needed' work and leaders will have huge time for strategic thoughts. This is quite true across the hierarchy ladder.

Planning skills – coaching needs to address the real skill set required, is a concern across leaders. Skill set needs grooming and training once understood which should ideally match with the personal and professional ambitions. Often leaders assume that too much of experience address all skill required for any business. Ideally it's incorrect. Skill orientation to growing dynamic business needs and preparing for the competitive edge is a definite need. Coaching needs addresses to find the right skill set for the development.

Mentoring Skills – Definitely mentoring skills would be essence of many positive outcomes. It would be the primarily skill set and subject matter delegation which the next in command would be needing for driving the same, for clarity again, mentoring is not coaching.

The next bunch of requirements like **communication skills, team building, faster bolder affirmative decision-making process, compassion and empathy, persuasion, interpersonal and**

motivational would be grooming of softer skills which are equally needed for every individual and its more of knowing what to do and how to do, rather than understanding and knowing what it is. Most of softer skills are assumed to already there and they would be implementing in their work, however studies have revealed it's a mere assumption. Various assessments, 260*, 360*, MBTI etc reflects on status and need a careful watch for evaluating any leadership assignment.

Top Coaching Needs for C- Suite and Seniors:

- ✓ Drive Vision
- ✓ Self-Awareness
- ✓ Creating Influence
- ✓ Leading as an example
- ✓ Leading Organisation in Crisis
- ✓ Strategy Focus at all Levels
- ✓ Decision – Speed and Correctness
- ✓ Team – collaboration and synergy
- ✓ Mentoring and talent mobilisation

Top Coaching Needs for Mid to Senior Managers:

- ✓ Motivation and Drive
- ✓ Conflict resolution and collaboration
- ✓ Drive results
- ✓ Multi-tasking
- ✓ Planning and execution
- ✓ Time and Work-Life Management
- ✓ Communication, Personal aura and Presentation
- ✓ Mentoring and Creating teams
- ✓ Empathy

Executive coaching for Maximising Impact at workplace:

HR and L&D team at any corporate would be working towards how the organisation shapes up to manage the above complexities and invest on people management skills to make the employees better prepared for the future challenges and dynamics.

Organisation would have their highest band for appraisal or their internal talent pool or knowing the next-in-line successors for leadership. The apex talent pool would also be aware of their challenges and the continuous pressure to keep learning and shaping for future requirements.

Executive coaching addresses to unleash your full potential and unlock all coachee's limiting beliefs and build pillars of conviction and self-regulation. Talents often remain dormant, coaching process helps to also uncover your own dormancy, reaching out to with your inherent strengths and pitching with your best potential which may be not known to organisation.

Shadow coaching:

Shadow coaching is an effective tool used with clients. It is a process of real time understanding of the coachee's daily schedule at work. Observe coachee at work place, observe the flow of events and the response of situations by the coachee. Coach gets a real time understanding on aspects like his/her communication, presentation, response to colleagues, prioritisation and may me sometime join at meetings on his responses to group. Coach can have a 360* understanding of the coaching needs and his/her alignment with the goal and expectation. Pointers which can be marked as non-discussed can be discussed later and looked at with better clarity to be better prepared to handle the action plan. It can be effective with:

- It's a real time understanding of what observed and what is conceived
- Unravel the real challenges, all facts are open and seen.
- Learning acceleration
- Observe various other behavioural patterns, communication which may be intertwined.
- Coachee can be given quick real time feedback
- Response for similar situation can be better prepared.
- Real time reflection and debriefing
- Collaboration challenges
- Stakeholder management

Executive coaching for Creating Talent Pool on Potential:

Executive coaching is being widely used by organisations across world for planning the leader pool. It creates a leadership pool which is planned not just on the appraisal outcome objectives but focus on potential and inherent capabilities. Talent management pool is a ready reckoner for candidate with new expansions of territory, product, vertical, smaller entities (SBU) within organisation, new verticals, leadership change.

Talent Management with coaching also addresses, coaching needs for leaders with new leadership changes, new inductees, competency improvement on certain core issues, team planning – bonding, new vision or it can address for gearing with motivation and big picture planning.

Executive coaching for Ensuring Higher Retention in organisation:

Lower retention can attribute various factors across which the coachee would be visualising. These needs to addressed faster. Clarity helps engagement. What does executive coaching provide?

- Engage with vision and larger picture with career aspirations
- Continuous learning and growing methodology, training and coaching
- Engaging for productive work planning using best productivity
- Mentoring for new and cross functional competency, employees
- Sharing a safe and secured workplace environment
- Work Life Balancing with new changing dynamics
- Diversity and Inclusion, Cultural and Dignity
- Work ethics, acknowledgements and rewards
- Empowering and trust
- Resolving conflicts and improve collaboration
- Managing millennials (would elaborate in subsequent topic)

Various customized strategies can be adopted for looking at higher retention with making coaching an ongoing process in the organisation and not a one-time intervention.

Executive coaching – Behavioural Coaching Model:

As defined earlier, this is a science of facilitating performance of individuals for their best productivity and address softer skills which otherwise may not be groomed with the training mechanisms. It emphasizes on a human mind understanding and response to a particular situation. It is not just a mental coaching but coaching with an integration of brain, body and mind.

Many of the coaching assignments are focussed on the behavioural coaching changes and is a one of the most requested coaching discipline by organisations. While this is valuable and needed for top executives, it is also very ideal for next-in-line leaders to shape up for future bigger opportunities.

But do senior leaders need to change behaviour? My answer and answer of many coaches is 'yes'. It is now researched that a small change of behaviour at top management can have greater impact on the output and financial results. At senior management, I am sure they would have experienced several training and leadership competencies but might have some blind corners which affect results and 360* feedbacks, behavioural coaching at that level is the necessary intervention for sustained change and yes, it is reflected at all levels and all ages irrespective of the positions and experience

Some process followed here:

i. Involving leaders in the coaching journey and develop clear understanding
ii. Ensuring leaders are aware of the feedback 360*
iii. Involve and acceptance of the behaviour which needs to be worked on
iv. Feedforward – collecting enough response across stakeholders for needed change they would wish to see
v. Plan a draft of plan – approach – process – change and review
vi. Use the change and have 360* on a specific duration, can be 6-10 months or annually.

Executive coaching – Crisis management:

Crisis management has been one of the most emerging topics of executive coaching. All organisation go through crisis and many more experience would have drawn during the covid pandemic. Analysis of crisis is an assumption which all leaders face or anticipate. Its critical coaching for future leaders and make them crisis ready.

Preparing for crisis is a great art. Many a time

- Crisis may not be there, its procrastinated
- Crisis may be there, but not aware
- Crisis may be there, aware but not prepared enough
- Crisis may be there, well aware and prepared to handle

Preparation for coaching during crisis, needs a real time data and facts for simulation. It's an assumption for a crisis and making the department, team , or organisation go through certain real time facts and analysis , brain storm their behaviour and finding the best action for finding an effective BCP – Business Continuity Plan . The coach challenges the coachee for information, assessment, elevates his/her mental and emotional responses and records the necessary actions. Coach would be prepared to effectively manage the crisis and make the leadership plan for 'what and how' they would face a real crisis.

Executive coaching – Boss as a Coach:

Quite interesting as the topic, itself. The journey of the Leader as a Boss to a Coach is an ideal transition and the most effective process internally within the organisation. Leaders across world have started seeing the value of coaching which is the direction of empowering rather than direction which is authoritative or 'do' orientation.

Previous chapters have elaborated on how the transformation can be discovered.

- ✓ Goals targets and KRAs can be discussed on how they are perceived and what's the effective thoughts around it, how team can be empowered, what to listen more deeply and assist on the process.
- ✓ What would be journey of team and their understanding on broad vision and company objectives. What are their alignment with personal goals and professional goals?
- ✓ What is required for motivation and drive for results, motivation coaching is a great tool for boss to take on the hat of being a coach
- ✓ Driving a positive outlook and negate the smaller hurdles
- ✓ Listening to them and aligning company strategy
- ✓ Coaching in the moment and help him/her solve the problem themselves
- ✓ Groom on the collaboration and team camaraderie

Boss can always take on the hat of being a coach now to see larger change or know fully well that the employee is being coached and would be seeking time and engagement session with boss to ensure he gets to answer his/her queries with boss.

Executive coaching – Use of assessments, tools and procedures:

Use of coaching assessments, type of assessment and the point of introduction of a particular assessment is entirely subjective and need based. Assessments have been used extensively across L&D, Coaching Organisations, Coaches , Assessment companies and Internal Tools to assess the coachee on various parameters and grounds of need . This is an evidence based, detailed and micro analysis of personal traits which is a reflection of the coachee in the coaching journey.

Coaching tools are very intricate, covers wide range of hard and soft skills, reflects on the status of the coachee on 'now' and 'what's the hidden potential or stimuli' to certain effects or simulation.

Assessments reflect on what is the natural instinct of the coachee and what can be the reflective, emotional, psychological responses on various attributes, various stakeholder, various simulation of challenges and leadership states.

While there are many types of assessments, mentioning some of most used in executive coaching process .

Assessment Types

Assessment Type	What does it focus on?	When can be used in coaching journey?
360* Analysis	Takes into account various feedback about the coachee from various stakeholders, peer, reporters, Seniors,	Should be ideally at Pre-Coaching session. However, the report can be used during various maturity

	Cross-functions	stages of the journey
DISC Analysis	Personality type and matching best of the DISC combinations	Pre-session or during the session when focussed on personality or collaborative challenges
Myers-Briggs Type Indicator	Personality introspection with psychological preferences – 16 quadrants understanding Extroverts-Introverts Sensors-Intuitive Thinkers-Feelers Judgers-Perceivers	Pre-session and during session on need
Marshall Goldsmith assessment	Leadership Excellence	During session, pre session
Hogan Personality Inventory	Personality understanding of leaders on the bright side. Has a predictive validity on 5 factor model?	Pre-session and during session on need
John Mattone Enneagram	Personality and strength finder	Pre session
Gallup Strength finder	Leadership assessment on the correct analysis of an individual – paired questions on thinking, believing and	During session / It can be previously done by organisation

	feeling	
Trust assessment	Leadership Dependability understanding	During session or interventions
Professional Dynamic Program PDP assessment	Leadership Skills and talent pool planning, leadership understanding in stress environment	During session or across by L&D for hiring, retention, team communication etc.
USC leadership style	Leadership skills assessment for leadership style Servant Front line Transformational Metamodern Postmodern Contrarian	During or pre session
Personal Interests, Attitude and Value Profile (PIAV)	Interest, value and attitude system Theoretical Utilitarian Aesthetic Social Individualistic Traditional	During session

Cognitive Assessment	Assessment of Intelligent Quotient, thinking, reasoning	Any point during the session in need
Locke and Latham, 1991	Goal setting up process and progress review	During session

It has been a growing trend of the number of different types of assessment and quite apt to various needs by the situation.

Assessment on crisis management readiness, artificial intelligence, team management skills etc and many such tools can be utilised for various personality and situations. Many assessments can be driven by HR team and data can be stored on annual basis and monitored progress. Efficacy and use of tools are absolutely on the coach as to when it should be utilised. Understanding of each tool, analysis of the outcome and the planning of action plans needs integration in the coaching session for the goal and action plan.

An overview of 360* assessment

360* as the name suggests gives an understanding of complete leadership. 360* opens up the assessment across all direct reporters, peers, supervisors, indirect reporters, self and others. This assessment gets a holistic understanding of 9 critical factors which defines any leadership and gives the horizontal and vertical depth of any personality and its leadership understanding. Recommended tool John Mattone – 360* assessment for Leadership.

Overall rating	**Critical Thinking**	**Decision Making**	**Strategic Thinking**	**Emotional Leadership**
Communica tion skills	**Talent Leadership**	**Team Leadership**	**Change Leadership**	**Drive for results**

Critical thinking – It's the objective analysis and evaluation for critical judgement. ***Coaching interventions for improvement*** – priority management, planning the simulation solution techniques for top priority issues, finding 2 or more ways to solve one particular problem, overcoming quick solutions or short cut methods and work for long term solutions, weigh the options and polarity mapping, track progress

- **Decision Making** – It's the process of working on various choices, work on various facts and figures, work on options and arrive at logical conclusion. ***Coaching interventions for improvement*** – Options and probable solutions will always have the good and flip side. Coaching should be to find out how a particular decision has cascading positive or negative effects, how it impacts the overall goal, how each smaller milestone adds or deletes the impact and what changes cannot be undone. Hence coaching process discovers this logic of arriving at best decision.

- **Strategic thinking** – It's the process of simulating one own mind to think beyond the visible solutions and forecast with clarity. ***Coaching interventions for improvement*** – multiple scenarios and complexity question handling, observation and reflection techniques, Cartesian questioning and coaching for leading visionary thoughts.

- **Emotional Leadership** – It's the ability to understand and manage emotions of self and others. Leadership key aspect as discussed was to be empathetic and hence should be aware of how it motivates and catalyse the whole scenario for active involvement of team and self towards goal. ***Coaching interventions for improvement-*** coaching for awareness at various levels, core purpose knowledge, empathy skills, self-management, social and cultural knowledge and management and drive high energy and motivation.

- **Communication skills** – It's your ability to convey not just words but purpose and intent with of your ideas and feelings. ***Coaching interventions for improvement-*** we have spoken of this several times in this book and many concepts would give clarity on how it can be improved on listening, positive intention, tonality, verbal and non-verbal gestures, active participation, adequate response and expressions, develop trust.

- **Talent Leadership** – One of the big drivers for leadership and most sought. It's the process to evolve the leadership aspect and groom benchmarks for being a role model across leadership traits. ***Coaching interventions for improvement*** – Model Leadership acumen, learning objectives and core values, think with purpose, realities and resource understanding, groom self and team, vision and road map

- **Team Leadership** – Refers here for being a team driver for results, moving self and organisation towards a shared objective. ***Coaching interventions for improvement*** – plan effective actions and check efficacy, collaboration, team relations, team motivation and learning, effectiveness and efficiency, win-win solutions.

- **Change Leadership** – It's the process of systematic approach to deal with transition and transformation of people, process, management ***Coaching interventions for improvement-*** being uncomfortable is comfortable, transition understanding and your role, methods and new skills, collaboration and communication, action planning and progress tracker, accepting the new normal.

- **Drive for results** – Most talked yet not an easy understanding. It's the persistent zeal to drive actions passionately with optimism. Results are not in control, only actions can be controlled. ***Coaching interventions for improvement-*** Strategy and direction with clarity, plan stretch goals, high motivation, speak for failures and success, trust and dependability, develop self and others, optimistic mindset, emotional balance.

How to ensure executive coaching succeeds in an organisation?

It is now well observed that executives do go through lots of training and grooming exercises and coaching interventions, despite this the overall organisational capability do not proportionally grow, what could be the reasons?

Coaching interventions are often focussed on the individual growth, often the individual would do his/her best to tune to new adoption of things which the environment does not support, encourage and give time. There may be a conflict as coaching culture needs to be imbibed across the organisation and not to few individuals or the coached employee should be given enough space, time to do the needful changes for own and organisational growth. Also change process isn't easy, Coachee need to be sure about what exactly would assist for growth, coach should be confided upon 100% and let the flow happen. HR and department should support the change process and allow the implementation. HR/ Department/ Other related functions should be equally responsible for the coaching process and reshape their roles and responsibility across organisation. Here coaching outcomes has to be understood on larger canvas of organisational betterment rather than an individual. As more employees are exposed, the overall growth and change is visible for success.

"The Goal is not to be better than the other man, but your previous self."

– Dalai Lama

Chapter - 8

Life Coaching

What is Life Coaching?

Life coaching primarily addresses people to progress in their personal life and achieve better fulfilment on their personal and day-to-day life. It addresses various subjects like relationship, career, health, happiness etc. Coach would focus on the conversation quite similar to the previous processes and identify the actual core issues which needs to be addressed and what's holding it back. Coaching plays a significant role and takes the coachee on the path of progress. As mentioned, it is a slow process as it gradually sinks in to change a particular way of thinking, some habits to go away with, some new process to adopt, garner a way of perceiving and reacting to various issues.

Many would be quite confused seeing various aspects of life coaching today, few expert life coaches can address

- Family relationship
- Peer and friend relationship
- Personal relationship
- Financial coaching
- Career coaching
- Spiritual coaching
- Work-Life balance coaching

- Diet – Health coaching
- Communication
- Confidence and presentation ability
- Being happy
- Facing challenges and adversities
- Creative coaching
- Fear and anger management

Now many would wonder the difference between how life coach would be different than counsellors or therapist or psychiatrist.

Please refer to the beginning of the coaching introduction where it is quite simple to gauge that a ***coach is not a medical practitioner*** and will not be able to treat any medical condition which needs a certified counsellor or therapist. Coach takes on from the place when coachee is 100% fit and ready to be coached and he/she understand the process. If the discovery indicates deep anxiety, irritation or a background of pain/sorrow/medical history, it is better to be referred to certified professional and is beyond the purview of coaching.

Life coach takes the process of discovering latent potential with a coachee and treads a process of doing things towards goal. Again, to repeat it is not a process of giving any advice, consultation, mentoring, therapy or counselling. This difference needs to be understood and expectation set early. The process is quite deeper to unravel 'your' discovery and work 'yourself' towards it, with coach a guide to travel with the journey.

What can you expect from a Life Coach

- ✓ Go into the self-discovery phase of finding your inner and outer core
- ✓ Start strengthening your strengths
- ✓ Take charge of your mind and control your responses
- ✓ See your personal goals start happening
- ✓ Moving away from your limiting beliefs
- ✓ Getting out of your comfort zone and plan your goals
- ✓ Finding my core purpose
- ✓ Prioritising my day with meaningful contributions
- ✓ Gratitude and acknowledgement
- ✓ Self-Management
- ✓ Accountability of self

Discover .... Discover...... Discover and Strengthen yourself

Facts from a Life Coach

- Coaching is a gradual process, some changes do take time
- All coaches vary on their niche and process
- Life Coach is not a doctor/therapist/counsellor and cannot treat mental illness

Simple yet powerful asks during a life coaching session:

Relationships

- What does relationship mean to you?
- What relationship do you think are valuable?
- What makes you feel happy about a relationship?

Health

- What are your top health goals ?
- What does health mean to you ?
- What have been your best achievement on health ?

Finances

- On a scale of 1-10 , what is your financial status ?
- What does wealth planning mean to you ?
- What is your debt mitigation plan ?

Career

- What are your career goals ?
- What have been happy so far on this mission ?
- What do you feel you should plan now ?

Goals

- What goals you plan to achieve in next 3 years ?
- What if you do not achieve the goals ?
- What would you feel happy 1 year from now ?

Happiness

- What makes you most happy ?
- What do you do to make yourself happy ?
- What do you do to make others happy ?

Time/Priority

- If you have to do one thing , what is that ?
- What did you do to find time for leisure ?
- How would like to see as a master of planning ?

Spiritual

- Where do you find solace after a sad moment?
- What makes you connect to your soul ?
- What would like to confess and feel better ?

Creativity

- How does a new idea excite you?
- What can you do to think differently ?
- How creative are you now on a scale of 1-10 ?

Life Coaching – How do I know what's my most important concern:

Please refer to my initial elaboration of **'Wheel of Life'**

It speaks about each goal on a scale of 1-10. Any human would have scores from 1-10 at various bands. Across all pie of career, life, family, relationship, fun, spiritual, social etc. coachee can be from level 1- level 10. Each can be further broken down and understood based on priority and urgent focus.

For Ex: Now let's see if we can have details further on career. What exactly you are looking to achieve in your career?

Career Wheel

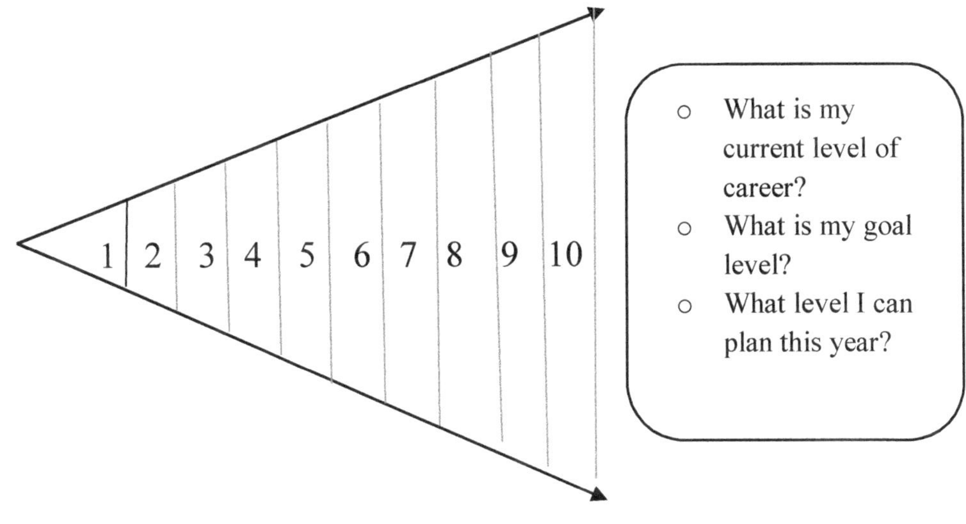

Assumption:

- Your current level is at 3
- Your goal is being at 10
- You can plan being at 7 this year
- You will plan being at 9 next year and 10 within next 3 years.

All wheel can therefore be broken down to 'spokes and each spoke can have various levels of current, desired and next desire with shorter time line. With the above assumption, assume you plan to be at 7 scale next year, so what are the questions which can be powerful enough to shape your travel from level 3 to level 7? What are your plans behind? What makes you believe the level 7 next year? Is it over planned or under planned? All such queries can be thwarted during the session and the plan of 7 or 'x' is more detailed with several big and small actions. Further spokes within career can be

- Professional career
- Aspirational career if any, i.e. I wanted to be a journalist, author etc. and so on and so forth.

We may be highlighting a particular problem or issue which bothers us often and we tend to showcase that as the actual deterrent for growth. Let us find out from this assessment:

Coaching Tool – 17. Self-Assessment

Sl.no.		Rate yourself on 1(Low) – 5(High)				
a	I feel I need to be always correct	1	2	3	4	5
b	My values, beliefs and thoughts are not expressed by me in my work	1	2	3	4	5
c	I am a materialistic guy and look for things which can make me happy with materialistic possessions	1	2	3	4	5

d	I remain upset with my financial conditions	1	2	3	4	5
e	I remain worried for my health, but can't allocate the time needed	1	2	3	4	5
f	I remain anxious planning my priority	1	2	3	4	5
g	I remain stressed out the entire day	1	2	3	4	5
h	I do not know what else I can do to be better	1	2	3	4	5
i	I aspirations are not met in my life	1	2	3	4	5
j	I often live a life of superficiality	1	2	3	4	5

Lower the score, you can now command your life. Higher the score, you know why you remain problem focused and get drifted away from purpose.

Coaching tool – 18.

Discovering more about self: Please try and discover yourself

What is that you always wanted to do but never been able to express?

____

What is that you never wanted to do and never want to express?

____

What is that you always wanted to do and have expressed but still not achieved?

____

What are your dreams and fantasies which you like to realize and see them?

____

What were the real reasons of your failures? Were you responsible for it?

____

What is that hypothetical truth that you live and do not let go off?

____

What are those truth of your life which you will never share with anyone?

____

Use of NLP (Neuro Linguistic Programming) in Life Coaching:

NLP has been one of most used and result changing intervention during coaching journey. It was developed by as early as 1970's by John Grinder and Richard Bandler. It has a series of techniques and procedures for understanding human behavior and their responses to success or failure. While NLP focusses on methods and strategy on decoding human minds, coaching is taking it forward to use NLP and further plan the strategy which can be used to build awareness and outcome. Coaching can be independently be done without use of NLP, this may be assumed to be an effective tool which makes the coach-coachee understanding faster and mastery of various techniques.

'NLP drives a positive change in your coachee every time'

To keep it simpler in this book, NLP has 3 main understanding:

1. **N** – Neuro, as it means, it is the use of the brain to understand various things that's happening around. 'What' you understand and 'How' you analyze is very important for knowing. It's very important to know and analyze it correctly
2. **L** – Linguistic, words or languages what you hear, how you hear and what you respond and speak. What influence words or language have on you or your words on others
3. **P** – Programming, it revolves around how these neuro stimuli, languages shape one's behavior. Your actions which is finally emerging is a response to the drive of your final outcome or results.

Some questions make us anxious and less confident.

- What is making you unhappy?
- What makes you so afraid now?

- What makes you feel insecure financially?
- What is your concern on health which disturbs you?

NLP Coaching process takes you out of these and makes you more confident, clear, optimistic and remove your phobias and limiting beliefs.

Top 10 benefits you can expect with NLP:

- Clarity of vision, purpose, values and your limiting beliefs
- Be more confident and make others confident
- Handle people with various types of personality
- New Ideas to overcome problems and think solution
- Your leadership attributes
- Improve your communication
- Develop and maintain good and strong relationship
- Work on better responses on your behavior
- Relax – can be calm after stress
- Slowly you can remove pain, fear, allergies, phobia

NLP supports few of the following during coaching

- **Presuppositions** – What I see or you see is different and applies to all, there is no definite mapping for a situation and hence all see every subject in their ways. Commonly, we do suppose few things like, my past and future is similar …on contrary it may not be, my future may be much brighter.

- **Framing - reframing** – It's like adding a frame to your thoughts as a picture and seeing it. The picture looks completely different. A particular situation, picture can look differently by changing the frame, till it matches with the content. There are deeper concepts built in this over a time and takes care of core transformation, perceptual positions, visualization, timeline etc. For example, a discussion can, be with a HR person to employee – 'Hi, lets discuss what you wanted to discuss in next 1 hour, its 10 am now and we should be over by 11 am. Around 10:50 am HR can always remind 'Hi, its already 10:50, you can focus on most important things now to make it most effective'. The focus is understood back as a frame was set at the start with a timeline. Another example – boss says 'look I can't do this for you' …it can reframe as 'look this is what I can now do at best'

- **Meta programs and models –** Meta programs are focused towards shaping our perceptions and models are to avoid generalization, deletion and distortions. For ex – 'no one appreciates my work' …how can somebody be sure …may be someone who does, and I am not aware. What is removed here is generalization. Another example – 'this work was simple and I was expecting from you'… was this really simple? Some more questions on meta -
  - What are you looking in your new job?
  - What is the reason you chose to do this?
  - How do you know you are doing a perfect job?
  - Who was your favorite boss? Tell me more about him?
  - Would like to know the bigger picture before you start the project?
  - Tell me more about what did you to celebrate your birthday?
  - After the event, what was your message to yourself?

- If someone called and asked you 'I need help' what would be your reaction. In case you don't know him/her, then what?
- When you fail, do you analyze or move ahead fresh?
- I am anxious – how do you know that I am anxious?
- I will be happy – what would make you happy about it?
- That's Ok – what makes you feel OK about it?
- They did not understand – how do you know about it?
- We can keep it ready – what exactly are you expecting?
- WhatsApp is a nuisance – which chats/groups exactly?
- Politicians are corrupt – Anybody in particular? What makes you feel so? Who are ones you feel so?
- In which direction do you think your career is moving?
- He keeps trying – In what ways? What makes you feel so?
- They gel well – In what ways?
- There is anger in them – Who's angry with whom?
- I want recognition – What exactly do you mean by it?
- I feel bad – In comparison with?
- He is hard working – Hard working than whom?
- You don't like me – What makes you feel so?
- My boss feels I am not contributing – Why do you feel that?

- Men who cry are not strong – Don't they have feeling? Who feels like that?
- Because of him I did that – What exactly did he do?
- He never understands – Never?
- He is like that – Like what?

Life Coaching – Coachee's state of mind (Matters of State)

It is an absolute pre-read of coachee's mental status and readiness for a session. As elaborated earlier, coaching should not start when the mental state of coachee is bad or not in a mood for proactive listening, reacting or responding. State of presence can be triggered by auditory or visual triggers. Coach should gauge the right trigger needed for steering the conversation to a desired outcome if response is adequate. State here is the emotional, mental, physiological condition at that moment. State can be changed, altered or paused. It is important that coach should understand the clarity and use the situation to trigger the right state.

For example –

1. ***Coachee comes with lot of anxiety and multiple thoughts***. Simple technique can be 'close your eyes for 5 mins, relax and breathe deep. Relax your thoughts, take deep breathes and relax all your muscles. Stay calm, breathe normally and focus on your breathe … slowly open your eyes'. The state of anxiety or hurriedness changes within minutes to calm. It may need more time and deeper mediation, but the effect is felt immediately and state is altered.

2. ***Coachee says I can't win this trophy and is shaky on thoughts.*** Power of visualization can be applied here. 'Close your eyes and imagine. Think about the trophy…. what is the trophy like? Now recall the days from when you started the urge to own it, win it. what all you have

done to get the same. Recall all the sweat and hard work…imagine you are sitting in the auditorium and you are the best contender of the trophy…. your name is called and you walk slowly to the dais …while you stand there…you see all are clapping for you…. You are super excited…you go ahead…hold the trophy…. feel it…kiss it and hold it high for all to click pictures…now you are called to say a few words…you move to the mike and speak; you thank all and recall all the hard work and the happiness. Imagine being the recipient and cheering… now slowly open your eyes…was the moment of truth beautiful? …do you want to miss the trophy by any chance' The state of uncertainty will surely be pushed back with huge rejuvenation and confidence to all the possible efforts now to see the real truth. This is a change of state.

Life Coaching – Coachee's response through V-A-K

All human respond and resonate with various senses. During coaching, coachee responds to various senses but few are observed significantly called VAK (Visual, Kinaesthetic , Auditory) . These are pure representational system of each person and coach need to understand and respond similarly. Smell and taste also play a factor but from coaching perspective the former 3 response needs to be understood. How do we gauge who's responding when?

- Visual – Coachee visualize faster and better, the picture is drawn the moment spoken, they are good creators and construct images fast.
- Auditory – Coachee is sharp on voice, words, tone, pitch and start interpreting differently. The context can be perceived in a different way.
- Kinaesthetic – Coachee expresses feelings and movement and they start dwelling on the response.

During a session, coachee would be using some phrase, words, non-verbal indications to clearly demonstrate his/her style. It is then as a coach, if similar words are reciprocated, coachee responds faster. The rapport making and discovery process becomes easier and is co-related. Some words which resonate these styles:

Visual :

1) I would like to **look** at things this way
2) He **looks shortsighted** to me
3) **Watch out** for bigger things
4) Did you **notice** the change
5) Would like to **view** the progress

Auditory:

1) That ***sounds*** good
2) I felt great ***talking*** to you
3) Did you ***hear*** the points
4) Let's ***talk*** on the same
5) I want to make this point ***loud*** and clear

Kinesthetic:

1) ***Hold*** your idea
2) Would like to ***go*** through
3) ***Keep digging*** for solutions
4) He ***walks*** the talk
5) Let's ***arrive*** at the point

All the above 3 representational styles can be reflected with similar answers, subconsciously the answers immediately start reflecting on a bond, rapport and good answers which moves the coachee to outcome.

During coaching you can also ***gauge your coachee style by seeing his/her eyes .*** This is very integral of a coach to understand the coachee style and his/her responses to various questions , each answer should not be looked with the content of the answer but the eye movement and the non-verbal emotions . A well trained coach can quickly judge the person and shape up various questions , solutions , words which reciprocate the emotion , feeling , construction , memory and forms a working actionable plan .

RIGHT SIDE **LEFT SIDE**

Imaginative / Constructive / Lie **Memory based / Facts / Truth**

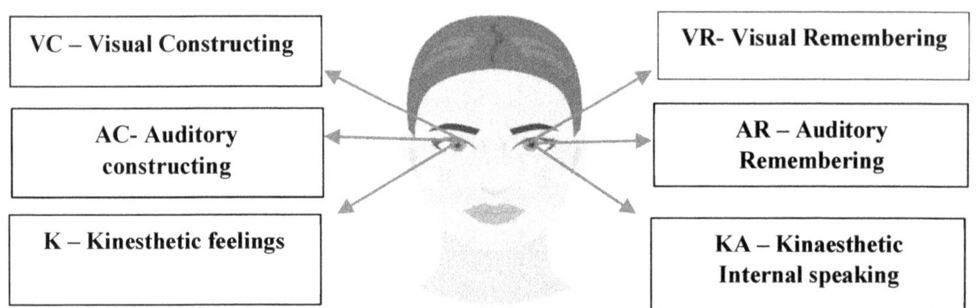

Knowing your style with eyes

So, what does the above signify? During coaching or any conversation, start looking straight to the eyes, eye lids and their movement. When a question is asked, where does the coachee's eye movement happens? The left side movement of the eye defines on facts and right-side focus on construction. Hence left can be assumed to be facts and truth and left is false or lie. The question makes him/her think or construct, remembering sounds, pics or feelings or asking yourself. This is a good foundation understanding to study human behavior, style and their responses to various questions.

Life Coaching – Spiral Coaching Model

An old concept but quite relevant to coaching parlance. Developed after the 2nd world war, Dr. Clare Graves had put forth this concept. This is to understand in simpler way, that what we needed for our growth a decade ago, may not be relevant now or a new approach is desired to change the same coachee, decade after. The representation of colour is a stage and fits into the coachee's thinking model. Please do not overstep to change the thinking process of coachee based on yours. During the process it is important that coach knows exactly the colour band and the thinking pattern. These are not stages but spiral thinking process and is inclusive of each code.

Code	Thinking pattern
Purple	*dependability, trust, warmth, gratitude, superstitious – seek safe zones*
Red	*courage, dominance, impulsive, power, egoistic – aggressive and power seeker*
Blue	*accuracy, conformity, prudence, duty, loyalty – seek detail and meaningful purpose*
Orange	*ambitious, uniqueness, wealth, materialistic, status – seek influence and drive for possibilities*
Green	*awareness, empathy, fairness, consensus, support – seek acceptance, harmony and inner peace*
Yellow	*agile, assertiveness, flexible, realistic, knowledgeable – seek understanding of complex subjects, collaborative*
Turquoise	*Calm, collective, holistic , content, tranquility – seek knowledge for harmony , peace, flow*

Remember, we have already emphasized that all coachee are complete and whole. While some of the above characteristic may not be the natural thinking of the coach or the mentor, conversation has to be built on the very fact that the above styles are the coachee's natural styles. Somebody may be very warm and seek safer working conditions, some may be very aggressive and ignore safety. Some may be very impulsive and aggressive where somebody would seek details and look for better purpose. Somebody may be assertive and solve difficult problems whereas some may be content and seek changes to happen naturally. These are what all humans are and we tend to have very unique thinking pattern and reflect the same in our professional and personal life.

COACHING CONVERSATIONS AND COACHING SITUATIONS

Chapter -9

Executive Coaching: Convert a simple hyper corporate conversation to coaching conversation.

Boss to team leader colleague on a month business:

Boss – John, meet me at my room.
John – Yes boss
Boss – It's a disaster, you and your team did nothing, we did miss targets.
John -Ys..yes...I know but...
Boss – What but .... your team was miserable, why didn't you achieve?
John – Boss, we managed around 90% target, but missed 10% due to some known reasons...
Boss – I do not want to hear these excuses. How many team members do you have?
John – Boss, 8.
Boss – Remove 2-3 if they are not working
John – But sir.... 3 are already down with fever, we did best with 5
Boss – Nothing doing, convey them I need to hit targets now, no excuses, bye.
John – Ok boss.

Now Boss as a coach
Boss – John, meet me at my room.
John – Yes boss
Boss – It was not a great month and I was expecting more, what made you miss targets?

John – Yes boss, me and my team feel bad after a good try on missing it.
Boss – Tell me more on what you and team tried?
John – Boss, we had put out few new initiatives like…………. Having understood that we have lesser team members, we put out best, however we still managed to do 90% with 5
Boss – What was the additional work your rest 5 members could add when 3 of the members were down with fever?
John – I am happy to tell you that each 5 members added…….
Boss – That sounds good but you still missed.
John – We realize and we have already done our planning better this month from beginning
Boss – What makes you confident this month?
John – Boss, this is my new approach ………and the lesson learnt ………. Would not be allowed, I am sure of not missing the targets
Boss – How can you track the progress?
John – We have scheduled intermittent reviews and………… and we will analyze gaps …… I am sure we will do well.
Boss – Are you confident on your approach this month?
John – Yes and thanks for your support always, would surely do my best
Boss – Ok thanks
John – Ok boss

I hope it was quite easy to differentiate the difference between the conversations, the former is used more often and the resultant effect is also obvious that John is fearful, worried and anxious for the current month in the same way. John is scared for new challenges and new efforts. In the later step, John and boss had a dialogue even when boss is angry and worried. The scope given by boss to John was more provoking what he could do better now. John is equally feeling bad and need not be pushed to a shell. He should be encouraged along with his team for productive thinking and efforts to make a full proof current month to achieve the business. The use of questions, asking John to think and articulating the same discussion in a coaching format, changes the tone and the outcome. Thus, coaching becomes effective and useful.

Coach and coachee converse on priority management:

Coachee: Hi Coach, wanted to talk to you on how I am finding it difficult to manage priority at work
Coach: We can surely meet on....
Coachee: OK
Coach: Ok, I heard you find priority management as a topic to discuss.
Coachee: Yes
Coach: What makes you think priority management as a concern for discussion.
Coachee: Yes, too many and multiple work has cropped up. I am supposed to complete all, I do not understand which to complete first, which to do later.
Coach: Ok, I understand. What would you feel if you can be successful in prioritizing your work?
Coachee: Just be happy there are no reminders and all work completed in time
Coach: Pause and think, do you have any options for working it out.
Coachee: After pause .... Yes, few work I have been doing which may be done by my team (person A) and some by (person B) but still I have to see all
Coachee: Wait...I recall, I was also tied up completing some work for the guy who was on leave.
Coach: That sounds good, what would you do to plan your pending work with each team member.
Coachee: I haven't spoken to them yet; I need to plan with them
Coach: What would be your first priority then?
Coachee: I think I should list down the pending work and segregate to each team member and I am sure I will delegate and also supervise.
Coach: Wow, you look to have a solution, will that work out as a solution?
Coachee: Looks good
Coach: What would be your supervision now to ensure all work is complete?

Coachee: I would now give a detailed plan to them and monitor progress based on first deadline to last; I am sure I can schedule it.
Coach: That's sounds good and you look confident
Coachee: Yes, also I feel lighter, lets catch up next week
Coach: Sure, I am sure you would have done good progress by then
Coachee: Yes, and thanks

The above conversation is to make the coachee aware of the situation and the options available, think on it and plan what can the best option now to work on, how to work on and what would be the most effective outcome.

Coach and coachee conversation on alternate career planning

Coachee: Hello good morning coach
Coach: Good morning ……
Coachee: I wanted to meet and talk to you my career planning, which has been bothering me. I do not know where I am heading.
Coach: Career planning, what makes you feel bothered?
Coachee: I feel career wise I had some dreams but I am going slow and do not know what next to plan and do
Coach: What was your dream career?
Coachee: I wanted to start my own business but am still stuck at my job, I love my work but I wanted to do my business and become an entrepreneur
Coach: That sounds very enterprising, what business had you been planning?
Coachee: I wanted to start a retail business on IT services as I have been in this field and I feel I can do well.
Coach: You look confident, then what is holding you back here?
Coachee: I do not have enough funds which is holding back.
Coach: Oh, funds would be needed for all business right, what would be the exact need
Coachee: I guess around ₹_____ would be a good start
Coach: What makes you sure about this amount?

Coachee: I have spoken to somebody but I am not sure.
Coach: What do you think you should do on this now?
Coachee: I recall, I have an ex-colleague who could tell me more on this.
Coach: Ok, what else can you do to find more details on it?
Coachee: I have been thinking of meeting few already established entrepreneurs on this and I have a friend who is also a finance guy, maybe he can tell me options.
Coach: That's wonderful, so what would you start with?
Coachee: Maybe I will start with meeting my friend, get an idea. Connect with one of entrepreneur also and meet the finance guy to find a cost plan
Coach: That's seems wonderful, how would you go about it?
Coachee: I will chalk out a plan now for next 7 days and try to get all the ideas as soon as possible, hope to be more aware by next few days.
Coach: Good thinking, I am sure you will.
Coachee: Some ideas are already striking me ...
Coach: What else you need to do to start your business other than funds?
Coachee: I feel I also may need some more skill set
Coach: Ok, what have you done on this?
Coachee: I have started this………course and this ……certification which will help me know more and start with all confidence.
Coach: already so many ideas are up and up is your confidence as well
Coachee: Yes, I feel so and I am raring to go with the start, thanks for your time and coaching me.
Coach: Thanks

The above conversation is for career planning, where the need to think on the lines is often avoided or delayed although the goal is clear. Working out exactly a few of the needful strategy, looking at possible solutions, working in detail on them, planning a timeline and reviewing the process is a great start.

Let's see the following conversations and what can be a modified coaching conversation.

Normal Conversation	**Coaching Conversation**
Do this today	*What can you do on this today?*
Why do you want to talk today?	*What do we need to talk about today?*
Is there any objective of our discussion today?	*What are the objectives of our discussion today?*
Did you think on your new assignment?	*What are your thoughts on your new assignment?*
Complete the work by Saturday	*What can you work on to complete by this Saturday?*
Can you start travelling today?	*What options do you have to start your travel from today onwards?*
Have you finished the task?	*What are the methods you working to complete the task?*
Start now	*What can you do to start now?*
Did you try?	*What have you tried so far?*
What's not going well?	*Can you tell me more on what is not going well?*
Why did you not fix the problem?	*What were few actions taken to fix up the problem?*
Can you commit now?	*What are you willing to commit now?*

Do it better this time	*What can be done better this time?*

On careful observation, it can be noted that any situational question can be modified to a coaching ask and the answer would be quite different to both the situation, keeping the content similar. The modified question has always better answers with thoughts.

Coaching Tool – 19.

Let us try to convert these to coaching asks:

Normal Conversation	Coaching Conversation
Do u know your work?	
Do you know i was expecting better?	
Why do I have to remind you?	
Where is your focus?	
Will you stop judging?	
When will you reach your goal?	
Where is my happiness?	

Let us use an example for the coaching model VISIONS® and study the flow

Example:

"I am worried, I want to be healthy".

VISIONS table has few questions which can help anybody to form the foundation process of the goal and attain an outcome. There can be several and different questions shaped up depending on the need and the outcome.

V – Visualization of your goals
I – Instill the Will
S – See your options
I – Initiate the actions
O – Overview the progress
N – Noting the natural flow
S – Sustain success

V	• What is that, you need to achieve? • What is your goal on health? • What do you want to achieve for your health? • What will make you happy for health?
I	• How important is health for you now? • What is keeping you so worried? • How committed are you for your health? • What makes you more concerned for health now?
S	• What are your thoughts to become healthy? • Tell me more on options you have worked on • What can you do now, keeping your hectic schedules?

	• What choices and sacrifices are you ready for?
I	• What are the actions can you work on now? • When can you start? • You said of half an hour of walking, what is the way you can be regular on it • What are you doing on diet this week?
O	• How can you start tracking your daily half an hour of walking? • What would be your daily check on calories? • When can you check your vitals? • Is there a planner which we can review of progress?
N	• What makes you sure now that you can extend to 1 hour of walking? • You would be glad on your diet, what makes you feel you can keep this habit and follow? • What would some other small steps you can take for being fit?
S	• Now that you look confident after 1 month, what can be your plans for next 3 months? • What can you do to reduce 20 kgs by next March? • Can you see now what can you plan to reduce your blood sugars and BP? • What would like to inspire others on your regime?

The entire flow of VISIONS completes the stages on what the coachee would be looking at with the answers and the subsequent related questions. Furthermore, let us relate to few situations and the related questions:

BUSINESS COACHING	• What is your business model? • Who are your target customers? • What does your business address to customers? • What is your product or service? • What are its advantages? • Who are your stakeholders? • Which is the most important feature compared to other competitors? • What is the outcome you are expecting in this year and next 3 years? • What are the investments planned? • How are you reaching out to your customers?

PROBLEM COACHING

- What is your problem which you would like to address?
- How important that problem is to your life?
- What is the way it is connected to your values and purpose?
- What is the background?
- When did this start affecting you?
- What were the barriers you had for this problem?
- Is this problem occurring often or once in a while?
- Is this really the problem or there is something more?
- What have you worked on this so far?
- How confident are you on a scale of 10 to plan to come out of it?
- What if the problem does remain?
- What options do you have now?
- What can be your best idea to solve it?

GOAL PLAN COACHING

- What is your GOAL now?
- What is that you want to achieve now?
- Tell me more on your goal?
- How did you arrive at this goal?
- What is that it makes this goal important?
- Describe the need to have this as a goal?
- What makes this goal in sync with your experience and qualifications?
- What does achievement of this goal mean to you?
- How would life be different on achievement of this goal?
- What are the various options which you may have to reach your goal?
- What are obstacles in reaching your goal?
- How can you see a goal which more specific details in it?
- How about planning sub goals?

LIFE COACHING

- What is the purpose of your life?
- What are your values?
- What are your biggest strengths?
- What is that which best defines you?
- When do you feel complete?
- What are your dreams which you feel to achieve?
- What are the things which make you happy?
- What are the things which makes you angry or irritated?
- Next year, what changes you would like to see in yourself?
- What does gratitude mean to you?
- Who all you would like to thank in your life?
- What does happiness mean to you?
- How do encourage others?
- Define yourself in one sentence?

MOTIVATION

COACHING

- What is your best ‘happy’ moment in the day?
- What do you do when you feel happy?
- What were your best and positive moments last year /this year?
- When did you last feel full of energy?
- How would you encourage yourself?
- Tell me what is the exact motivation you are looking for?
- How would your being motivated, motivate your family and friends?
- What can you do to motivate others?
- What benefits do you see, feeling happy and excited?
- What can trigger your happiness?
- What stops you from being happy?
- What can you do today to feel energized?

DECISION MAKING

- What is the background for this decision?
- What are the advantages and disadvantages on this decision?
- What makes you so sure about this decision?
- How is this decision aligned to your vision, values and thoughts?
- What are the things that cannot be undone later post this decision?
- What are your checks and balances on this?
- What is the feedback of other members on this?
- What fears or pressure can you remove before taking this decision?
- What will be most important change post this decision?
- What are the other expected/unexpected decision you may have to take again post this?

WELL BEING COACHING

- The way you are leading your life, what is the way you look at your well-being 3 years from now / 6 years from now?
- What types of food you love which adds more calories?
- What is your BMI? What have you been doing on it?
- Describe your daily routine? How much time are you able to concentrate on some exercises?
- What is your sleep routine?
- What does it take for you to stop taking cigarettes/alcohol?
- What is your feeling of having a perfect health?
- What are the lifestyle changes you can plan for better health?

RELATIONSHIP COACHING

- What were the change of things you noticed/observed in the behavior?
- Can you reflect on the smaller incidents which could have led to this?
- Describe the exact situations?
- What was your interpretation of those incidents?
- I could hear your love and compassion, what all do you do to make such a great bonding?
- What are the feelings you carry about him/her?
- Looks you are hurt too, tell me more on your attempts to douse off the spark?
- What would you do to avoid a similar situation in future?
- What are the ways can you keep up the good relation and nurture it ?

PERFORMANCE COACHING

- What does performance mean to you in your work life?
- What does achievement of your plans/goals mean to you?
- Describe on your best achievements so far?
- Can you tell more of events/situations where you felt you could have done better?
- What strategies have worked for you so far?
- What are the various options you can focus on?
- If you have to shortlist few actions, can you describe your top 3 actions now?
- What help do you seek from your seniors?
- What training or skill set you feel as an intervention required to better?

COACHING DURING PANDEMIC

- What has been your biggest learning during these times?
- What were your best preparations to handle crisis?
- What would like to see yourself as post the pandemic? (1-2 years)
- What better can you plan and do during and after the situation?
- What were your skills, knowledge addition during these times?
- How would be those skills and talents better be used for your personal and professional work?
- Who all are your grateful during these times?
- How would like to see yourself better prepared next time onwards?
- How can you see yourself prepared stronger in such eventualities?

SPIRITUAL COACHING

- What does spiritualism mean to you?
- What is your realization when you know about doing a mistake?
- What has been your life's best learning which you would to pass to next generation?
- How do you connect with your heart and mind when taking a bold step?
- What makes you hear your intuitions while taking such decisions?
- How would you describe peace and happiness in your daily life?
- What does joy of giving mean to you?
- When you grow old and you have to look back at a younger you, what advices you would surely give?
- What regrets you would like not to have at the end of your life?

Coaching tool : 20.

Let's try to ask coaching questions on 'how can I better myself?'

- ____
- ____
- ____
- ____
- ____

MORE QUESTIONS

- What's going on, dear friend?
- What's in your mind?
- What's you're feeling now?
- What is your real need?
- What's a perfect life?
- What's a perfect partner?
- What is the better expectation?
- What is the goal we can work on today?
- What would you like to accomplish?
- What has worked in our meeting?
- What has to be added to make meetings more useful?
- What is the goal of our life?
- What is an ideal result?
- What is the outcome expected of our coaching conversation?
- What is the one advice you would like to share?
- What is the one learning you would like to give?
- What is the one lesson you will pass on to your kids?
- What priorities can define your work better?
- How would like to elaborate your efficiency?
- What are the new goals for the year?
- What were the learnings of the last year?
- What are the mistakes you would not like to repeat?
- Assume to be an Olympic winner, what is the schedule you would put for yourself?
- What is the one thing you would like go away with?
- What is the one thing, you feel should be discouraged while planning?
- What is the benefit of success for you and family?
- Is your goal SMART?
- Does your plan have a timeline?
- What is required to shorten the time period?
- What are your inhibitions?
- What intuitions drive your thoughts?
- Can you summarize what actions you would like to take now?

Phrases which can be used to share during coaching:

To establish focus	*Let's refocus on the objective* *What would be the core area to concentrate?* *Assume the worse outcome, what would be the focus now?* *Let's change the focus now* *If this isn't helping, can you focus on what can help?*
To encourage	*Your confidence is immense* *Your efforts would surely bring wonders* *I am sure you have all the abilities* *Things will get better now* *Look ahead and give your best*
To bring awareness	*Tell me more about this.* *If you do this, what can be the outcome* *Between these options, why are you looking at this?* *If you are the boss, what would have been your thoughts?* *What's the one thing that is pulling you back?*
	I know what you are going through *I can feel for you*

To empathize	*The time will change for good* *Don't worry, this shall pass away* *You must have gone through such difficult times*
To challenge	*You should not run away from this* *Please face the situation as it is* *What's the great point doing this?* *Your analogy may not be welcome?* *You assume something, without actually doing* *Don't you feel you should stop doing this?* *I see you are not open to new thoughts* *This way, our goal looks difficult*
To reinforce thoughts	*Your ideas look good, can you elaborate?* *You can do it, think more* *Let's dwell on this option* *This strategy sounds weak, do you feel so?* *What if have only one way, what is that?* *You seem to be afraid of this, what can make you stronger?*
	What values make you proud? *What are your happiness triggers?* *What is your strength which you can*

To discuss on strengths	*speak for most?* *How would you encourage others?* *Think basic and try simple solutions* *One change you would do make your weakness to strength*
To push for actions	*Have your started on with the action?* *Now please do it* *What is the one step today you can take?* *If you haven't taken action yet, when can you do next?* *Do not expect changes without taking actions* *Actions will now speak better* *You will changes post taking this action*
To help decision	*If you are to decide, please start now* *What if you do not decide* *What can be the worse out of this decision?* *Have you thought of the various hurdles post taking this decision?* *How can you see the decision going in your favor?* *What decisions can help you overcome this?*

"Failures are opportunities for your best learnings, use them as your weapons for success"

- Self

More on Coaching discoveries and Coaching tools

Chapter -10

Coaching Millennials – Must at Workplace:

(Published on LinkedIn)

By 2021-26, 75% of the Global workforce will be millennials across most Industry, India also would see 66% and above in the same space with more than 40% of population who are young.

In the next five years, more than half of the workforce will be made up of the millennial generation. This generation has changed and influenced almost all aspects of the IT , world-politics, media, communication, and business. This generation is continuously marching towards change while driving growth for organizations around the world. Millennials have entirely influenced the way businesses to innovate, market and engage with customers.

Millennials in the Workforce

Millennials are the fastest-growing workforce segment and the least understood. The search for purpose-driven work - Millennials appreciate and work for organizations that function as social enterprises and businesses that do not operate just for profitability towards C-suite executives and stakeholders. Millennials look for respect, culture and the right environment where the managers groom employees. They stick around such organizations. **Millennials have been dubbed the most 'impatient generation' in the workplace, with over 90% wanting 'rapid career progression.'** "According to our survey almost 60% of workers have experienced intergenerational conflict in the workplace. As Millennials make up a growing part of the workforce, finding a way for members of different generations to work together effectively is an increasingly high priority."

Where coaching can help

Millennial workers want their jobs to be meaningful and challenging, and its absence could impact their satisfaction in and intention to stay at their current position. Challenges which are epitome on any Millennial 1) Workplace Culture 2) Faster Progression and Appreciations 3) Growing Need for Better Take home 4) Transparency 5) Exposure to best learning 6) International Assignments and Engagements 7) Stress due to extended job hours 8) Job Satisfaction 9) Interpersonal Relations 10) New Tech Orientation and adoption. While challenges are many, few of the above are frequently reported for and needs to have a coaching journey to lead a process of change and better engagement and productivity.

To start with employees have been going through major changes of stress and psychological distress. They have been abundant with information and continuously seek new vistas of learning. It's no more about putting a blame of one's goal and desires vs what he or she is going through or their plans vs actuals. It's a trans phase of their journey where they need to find an anchor and bind their thoughts to directed actions. Millennials are a workforce with highest creativity with highest dynamicity. Coaching millennials have been tough with the initial phases are to calm down the thoughts, plan the career development, match skills and competencies with opportunities, planning of a road map which is realistic and achievable. It's a great assimilation of the physical, mental and emotional congregation with realities.

Self-Management Skills are vital because it helps enhance personal skills (such as delaying gratification and communication skills), work engagement, and self-goal setting. Proper coaching for Goal Setting in Personal Life are key ingredients for growth.

Thinking with a solution in mind another significant advantage of coaching for both the millennial employees and their employers is that it is based on a solution-focused approach.

Setting Personal Road Map with Milestones which are clear, practical and matching personal and professional aspirations may be the key outcome for seeing a sure progress during the Coaching journey. Unlike organizational changes, which focus on the external aspect or symptom of the problem, coaching addresses its root cause by focusing inward on the millennials' attitudes and emotions that impact their reactions to the situation. Through coaching, millennials can acquire a higher level of self-knowledge and personal responsibility concerning a self-directed personal plan, which can be applied not only to their professional lives but also to their personal lives. Organizations, as a result, gain an engaged and committed pool of young and talented employees.

What can a coach do while coaching millennials?

- Help discover core values and beliefs
- Give a safe and boundary less thinking space
- Encourage various 'out of the box' solutions
- Speed up the process as short-term achievements are sought
- Bring in the current realities
- Formulate SMART goals
- Coach to help discover the reskill and upskill needed

- Mindful coaching across all life spaces of finance, health, relationship, career, aspirations etc
- Continuously track progress

Summarizing: It's becoming very evident and important for the way Corporate and Workplace has taken Millennial and handled them. CX Executives 'Next' Planning, Performance Issues, Strategic Intervention for Coaching has majorly focused on Senior Leadership. It's time we realize and wake up to constantly Coach the Next-Gen for the Best output which the industry expects.

Why small and medium business groups need coaching, more than large business groups.

Small and medium businesses are those which are run with smaller teams who are more focused on the end results of business objectives and would be most of the time focused on the reactive time with all employee and focus on end results. Employees do multi-tasking and would be geared for several drives and would lose focus on the people and goal management. Reasons why I do feel, coaching needs more focus on these organizations, entrepreneur teams for the following reasons:

- **Stick to the core purpose of the company**: Most of the time, organization has several blue prints and thoughts before start of the organization. Now it can be a small business or a medium business. During the 6months – 3 years cycle, often the survival and continuation becomes utmost and some of the core purpose, objective and goals are overlooked or missed. It tends to drift away from the core plans which was based on some values, thoughts and objectives. Bringing the focus back with coaching, setting your goals, aligning goals to every work done in the organization and reflecting on the status of achievement gives a recurring success for a solid foundation.

- **Response to the stakeholders**: For the growth of the organization, employee tend to complete the task and respond as per their best capability. This coaching book does reflect a lot on what to listen, how to respond and react to various asks of stakeholders. Coaching takes through the process with details to make each employee more equipped to respond to the best which is required , appreciated and gives additional business . Here it's a personal coaching which dwells separately with each employee and not necessarily a general training.

- **Personal accountability:** Each employee faces multiple challenges and would be eager to do innovation, multi-tasking yet keep growing. Self-growth becomes evident and need grooming on the 'what better ways it could have been?', or 'what next I can plan reducing the time?'. Deliverables expected needs huge accountability along with hectic schedules, coaching does reflect on the top priorities, what, how and when and takes the goals through a realistic road map.

Systemic Team Coaching: Coachees post the coaching assignment, when they are on their own and in their own environment, sometimes slow down and aren't able to sustain the new normal. Systemic coaching is a fairly a new concept where it is concept to coach person, teams or system in a interdependent relationship. Here coach is co-creating insights for a sustained positive change. Now how is it different from traditional coaching? Each individual would be having personal goals and personal strengths, systemic coaching does not only focus on individual but the organization or team in whole or completeness. The enhances the organization's output by addressing the team collective strength and individual strengths, thereby creating a larger positive and sustained output. Systemic coaching addresses teams and focus on:

- Here the team is addressed as a complete one unit and aligns with the organization's goals, thereby also aligning individual goals to the organization's need and creates a synergy
- It fosters on individual smaller goals and interlinks on the team's goal which in turn reflects on the organization's goal.
- Each team member is vital entity to a larger entity and hence each member's outcome is important to the team's alignment and effect, therefore it focuses on both micro and macro picture

The need is very clear. Systemic approach addresses few larger aspects of any organization and hence being very popular

1. It aligns a huge collaboration across teams in organization which in practical has been a grey area
2. It quickly aligns to setting standards both internally within the organization but also aligns to the external environment
3. Preparedness for any exigency, uncertainty
4. Align team for current needs, plan for innovation for tomorrow and go all out of 'out of box' thinking for a longer sustenance

Difference between team and group coaching: Groups are people joining together for common interest, teams are people who work together with a shared objective. Team coaching can be a project team focused on relation, processes and team engagement.

Coaching Tool – 21.

Are you a good listener? Please rate yourself.

Sl.no.		Rate yourself on 1(Low) – 5(High)				
a	I give full attention to the coachee while he/she speaks	1	2	3	4	5
b	I do not keep any other distractions like computer/mobile or any other visitor when I listen to coachee	1	2	3	4	5
c	I respond with the coachee with 'yes', I hear..'etc	1	2	3	4	5
d	I like to listen to all the details , facts	1	2	3	4	5
e	I don't go with the discussion with my pre-fixed agenda	1	2	3	4	5
f	I can recall the points said during the discussion and can reflect on it at any point during the discussion	1	2	3	4	5
g	I make right non verbal gestures , like 'nod' or 'hands or body movement'	1	2	3	4	5
h	I do not interrupt until the coachee completes the statement	1	2	3	4	5
i	I ask questions and ask coachee to detail more wherever required	1	2	3	4	5

j	I know how to rephrase the entire statement and take coachee confirmation of same level of understanding	1	2	3	4	5

Scoring Indicator :

A score above 40 is a good listener , above 45 is a very active listener .

Coaching Tool – 22.

Are you a good communicator? Please rate yourself.

Sl.no.		Rate yourself on 1(Low) – 5(High)				
a	I always start with a greeting while I respond to both online or offline communication	1	2	3	4	5
b	During interactions, I plan and give enough time for the speaker to speak and I pay all attention and importance during it	1	2	3	4	5
c	During written/verbal communication, I pay enough attention to ensure I am empathetic	1	2	3	4	5
d	I often reach out to people (friends , colleagues, family) in good and bad times and extend support	1	2	3	4	5
e	I encourage and participate in discussions to give chance to everyone to express their views and feedback	1	2	3	4	5
f	I am confident before an important meeting to convey my points and express my views	1	2	3	4	5

g	My communication clarity gives my team , collegues , family enough knowledge and needful actions to be done	1	2	3	4	5
h	I discuss both success and failures and encourage my team for plan for future actions	1	2	3	4	5
i	I encourage discussion of goals and progress at intervals for bringing team and myself awareness and preparedness	1	2	3	4	5
j	I encourage atmosphere of learning and growth and I participate along with	1	2	3	4	5

Scoring Indicator :

A score above 40 is a good communicator .

Coaching Tool – 23.

What is your DISC - PERSONALITY? Please tick applicable box

A		B		C		D	
Aggressive	☐	Talkative	☐	Loyal	☐	Analytical	☐
Risk Taker	☐	Impressive	☐	Steadiness	☐	Oblige	☐

Energetic	☐	Emotional	☐	Trusting	☐	Focus on details	☐
Strong Will	☐	Persuasive	☐	Loyalist	☐	Compliant to rules	☐
Quick Decision	☐	Humane	☐	Empathetic	☐	Introspective	☐
Habit to Push	☐	Inspiring	☐	Patience	☐	Disciplined	☐
Tough	☐	Impulsive	☐	Good Temperament	☐	Facts and figures	☐
Direct	☐	Populist	☐	Respect people	☐	Accuracy	☐
Impatient	☐	Enjoy focus	☐	Good listener	☐	Careful	☐
Super Active	☐	Optimistic	☐	Good communicator	☐	Peaceful	☐

Scoring Indicator:

A – D (Dominant)

B – I (Influential)

C- S (Steadiness)

D – C (Conscientiousness, Compliance)

Column which has maximum (ticks) is your dominant personality, the next highest number of (ticks) is your second most dominant character. All characteristics are good and each traits needs better understanding of what can be the areas of improvement and communication styles of yours and matching ways with your coachee or speaker which needs tuning for best results

Coaching Tool – 24.

How good are you to manage conflicts? Please rate yourself.

Sl.no.		Rate yourself on 1(Low) – 5(High)				
a	I try out ideas even if sometimes I am not convinced	1	2	3	4	5
b	I include team/people/friends/family wishes to make them happy and included	1	2	3	4	5
c	In arguments, I discuss on both sides on pros and cons and take logical conclusions	1	2	3	4	5
d	I find happy to solve conflicts when I know the solution will benefit both the parties	1	2	3	4	5
e	I give opportunity to opposing people/sides to speak their sides and arrive at the final solution	1	2	3	4	5

f	When my view point is contested, I fight to get it accepted in some way or the other	1	2	3	4	5
g	I always try my best to win an argument	1	2	3	4	5
h	I keep my view point to myself and avoid open discussion	1	2	3	4	5
i	I feel wasting time convincing people my ideas and view point	1	2	3	4	5
j	I try and take a mid-path for problems to avoid conflicts to go on	1	2	3	4	5

Scoring Indicator :

The higher score in the questions demonstrate the following characteristics :

Questions :

a,b-accommodating | c,d,e-collaborating | f,g-competing | h,g-avoiding | j-compromising

Coaching Tool – 25.

GOAL PLANNING WITH VISIONS

V – Visualization of your goals

I – Instill the Will

S – See your options

I – Initiate the actions

O – Overview the progress

N – Noting the natural flow

S – Sustain success

Please write details as per your goals

V	My Goal No. 1	
I	Why its important and needed?	
S	What are my options/resources/ means?	
I	My actions (major and minors)	
O	What is my review period, how I am checking it?	

N	Do I need to change tracking periods/ How I am accepting the changes / What more can I do?	
S	How I am implementing the learning with other goals / a new milestone in the existing goal	

Coaching Tool – 26.

GOAL PLANNING WITH SMART

Please write details as per your goals

S	Specific goal	
M	How do i measure	
A	Is the goal achievable / what skill, resources need to be built/ action plans	
R	Is this realistic/relevant, matching my vision?	
T	When can i plan to reach?	

What can I ‘let go off’/ Stop for my actions	

Action Plan	Complete by	Review Date / Progress
1.		
2.		
3.		

References and Gratitude:

- *The Bhagawad Gita*
- *International Coaching Federation – ICF journals and press releases*
- *John Mattone – his thoughts and his books 'Intelligent Leadership'*
- *'Co-Active Coaching New Skills for Coaching People towards Success in Work and Life' by Luara Whitworth, Karen Kimsey-House, Philip Sandahl*
- *Coach Us Essential Coaching Tools Your Complete Practice Resource by Inc. Coach U ,The Life Coaching Handbook by Curly Martin*
- *Paul.J. Mayer -Wheel of Life*
- *Sandra L. Davis, D. Douglas, McKenna, Assay and Lambert, Bergin and Lambert – Psychologists and their journals*
- *John Medina 'Brain Rules', Timothy Gallwey- 'The Inner Game of Tennis' , Icon Border – Coaching Funnel ,*
- *Psychiatrist Elisabeth Kubler- Ross on grief cycle*
- *George Gurdjieff, Oscar Ichazo - Enneagram*
- *Effectiveness of leadership coaching An integrated evaluation framework by Hofmans 2015*
- *Executive Coaching for Results The Definitive Guide to Developing Organizational Leaders by Brian O Underhill, Kimcee McAnally, John J Koriath, Richard J Leider, Marshall Goldsmith*
- *Coaching Competencies and Corporate Leadership by Tracey Weiss, Sharyn Kolberg , Feedforward concepts by Peter W. Dowrick, Marshal Goldsmith*
- *Development Dimension International Inc – Learning modalities for leaders*

  Advancing Executive Coaching Setting the Course for Successful Leadership Coaching (J-B SIOP Professional Practice Series) by Gina Hernez-Broome, Lisa A. Boyce ,The Coaching Manual The Definitive Guide to The Process, Principles and Skills of Personal Coaching by Julie Starr

Thank you, readers, for your time

www.ingramcontent.com/pod-product-compliance
Ingram Content Group UK Ltd.
Pitfield, Milton Keynes, MK11 3LW, UK
UKHW022027190726
13853UKWH00005B/2141

9 789354 726293